Refrain

from the

IDENTICAL

Insight and Inspiration for Creative Eclectics

By

JoDee Luna

Cover Photo by JoDee Luna and Gina Marie Wilson
Illustrations by Gina Marie Wilson

ISBN: 1451577354
ISBN - 13: 9781451577358
Library of Congress Control Number: 2010904507
CreateSpace, North Charleston, South Carolina

DEDICATION

I dedicate this book to the creative eclectics in my family and among my friends. Thank you for fanning the fires of inspiration in my heart, mind, and soul through your examples of daring to live differently.

TABLE OF CONTENTS

INTRODUCTION

*"My artist wants to play, and I fear she will
embarrass me in public if I do not let her!"*
                                        -JoDee Luna

We live in a culture that extols the professional artist, educator, actor, and writer. Although we cannot help but admire the expert who achieves brilliance beyond our wildest imaginations, this book is for us *little people*; those who may never shine among the brightest of this world's stars, yet still have passions for personal expression percolating inside. The validity of our creativity does not rest upon laurels of fame or fortune. We should create merely because we desire to do so.

Everyone's journey through life is unique, but we creative eclectics seem to travel an especially perplexing passage. Our happy, though sometimes tortured souls, look with longing at those able to devote a lifetime to one pursuit, wishing we had the focus and wherewithal to follow suit. However, our varied interests in a plethora of art forms keep us dabbling in this and that. Like steering a chariot pulled forward by multiple horses, we attempt to hold all of our creative reigns in only two hands. Reconciling our scattered natures and channeling our diverse creativity often results in a somewhat splintered psyche.

As an educator and professional development trainer, I face the daily challenge of pursuing a demanding career while simultaneously nurturing the artist within that is struggling to emerge. I chose my career field because I have a passion to help young people be all they can be, yet I am a woman full of book ideas, artistic projects, and innovative technology. While I am devoted to helping my students discover their talents, there is an adolescent inside longing for my own time to create.

This book is a gift to those who are trying to understand their eclectically creative souls. I write it for artistic types who wish to reconcile this tug of divergent desires. I like to think that divine destiny played a role in my decision to publish this book. After seeing the website url www.refrainfromtheidentical.com in a dream, the idea to design a creativity website was born. Soon afterwards, the desire to publish a book on eclectic creative living sparked within. This initiated a process built upon the purposes and passions of my entire lifetime. Little did I know how arduous the process of bringing this dream to fruition would prove, especially for someone like me, who has such diverse creative interests.

Over the years, I have found it difficult to maintain only one interest at a time. My inherent inability, or lack of desire, to focus on a sole art form, or particular pursuit produced tremendous consternation as to whether I should have specialized in one particular passion. In those times of doubt, I questioned whether I should have developed my classical guitar skills instead of diversifying in several kinds of arts and crafts. I second-guessed my career choices—sometimes wondering what I could have accomplished if I had pursued a doctorate degree in education. At times, I threw myself into artistic activities in attempts to forget about disappointing circumstances and relationships.

Some have jokingly referred to me as a "Modern Renaissance Woman" because of the vast and varied experiences I have had throughout my lifetime: small-town country girl, world traveler, missionary, ministry leader, pastor's wife, businesswoman, teacher, professional development trainer, writer, artist, musician, dancer, and web designer. With this diverse background in mind, another purpose of this book is to offer an array of ideas, inspiration, and resources for people whose love for life drives them to sample many different forms of creativity.

I could wallpaper a room with all of my past artistic projects and business ventures; not to mention the many innovative ideas within me that still await exploration. Yet, the common thread throughout all of the years is that life turned out to be far different than I ever intended or anticipated. Often I have felt like one of the children of Israel wandering through the desert. God provided manna and direction one day at a time, while I grumbled about why I could not seem to figure out my destiny.

If I could impart truth to my readers, it would be to plan with an open mind because opportunities will come your way. We often look for that great high calling or sublime mission in life, but there's great joy and worth in just using your God-given gifts whenever you find the time and opportunity to do so. I rise and write every morning in order to discover what adventures await the day. As I now enter the last half of my life, a commitment to look for everyday miracles replaces youthful ambitions. What emerges is the desire to make a difference through following my God-given gifting.

Spending time with people and exploring what I love holds the most appeal and eternal value. I try to slow down in order to appreciate small, yet powerful surprises. A scribbled note from a student to express her feelings about a grade warms my heart. A struggling reader handing me a sketch of his guitar makes me desire to play my own neglected instrument. I live for the gleaming smiles of youth as they explore the joys of sculpturing before the holiday break. Watching them learn to master reading and writing makes my life worthwhile.

I organized this book with busy career people in mind who have limited time to read or explore creativity due to fulltime work. Each reflection is short and readable in one sitting. I wrote the reflections during early mornings before work, evenings after work, weekends off, and school holidays. It is my sincere hope and prayer that this book will serve as a companion to others needing encouragement along life's quirky creative pilgrimages. Although your experiences will most definitely differ from mine, perhaps the writings will impart faith and purpose as you discover and pursue your own creative journey. I encourage you to live to the fullest as you "refrain from the identical."

POWER TO THE LITTLE PEOPLE

Power to the little people
Roaming the earth
In search of creative expression
A safe place to call their own
Room to expand innovative ideas

Corporations and organizations
May control the world
But no one can master the human spirit
Save God alone
Yet, He chooses to inspire

-JoDee Luna

Chapter I

Exploring the Creative
Eclectic Temperament

*"Some people are blankets made out of one solid piece of material,
while others are quilts with a whole bunch of pieces sewn together."*
                                                          -Andrea Luna

Confessions of a Creative Eclectic

"Hi, my name is JoDee and I'm a creative eclectic."
      "Hi, JoDee."
"My last fix was...well...this morning."

If I imagined a twelve-step support group for people like me, I would call it "Creative Eclectics Anonymous." We are artistic types who thrive on sampling many art forms not as a living but as a lifestyle. (Although a living would be nice!) We dabble in multiple mediums, thriving on a little bit of this and that, yet not fitting into the conventional worlds of publishing, art, entertainment, or education. Creative eclectics may also be avid writers who confess, "I have a book in my heart..." Yet, if we stacked the amount of unpublished work residing in our journals and computers, it just might reach the ceiling. We spread ourselves thinly over creative toast, leaving inevitable dry spots due to insufficient hours in the day. Admittedly, most of us never take any design to market or book to press. We live "overwhelmed" as we "bounce around," loving the unique.

If you relate with any of the following descriptions, then you might be a creative eclectic (or want to become one):

I'm fed up with others telling me to focus.

People wonder if I have an attention disorder.

I can't seem to finish cleaning one room without being distracted by a mess in another one.

When I filled out my Facebook profile page, I listed multiple items in the hobbies category.

I've been known to make people's dogs nervous (or parents, friends...) because I bounce from one activity to another.

I like to have multiple creative projects so I can choose as my mood changes.

Don't make me choose just one kind of creative pursuit because I could not.

If none of those statements seemed to fit, read along with me and see whether any of my personal history resonates with you.

I am a creative eclectic personality type. I enjoy everything from dancing to digital design. "The Jack of all trades and master of none" description fits me just fine, and I am not ashamed to admit it, at least not during this season of my life.

My mother set my creative genetic code by turning every day into a magical experience of seeing beauty in her surroundings. Her talents were, and still are, incredibly varied and vast. Growing up, I remember her cooking five-course dinners like a skilled chief, trimming rose gardens for optimum bloom, harvesting and canning from garden and fruit trees, painting in various forms, sewing all of our clothing, crocheting a variety of items, knitting cozy scarves, crafting needlepoint designs, sculpting with dough, playing the guitar, and even belly dancing. Of course, this list is by no means exhaustive.

I grew up in a home where creating was as normal as breathing. Warm memories fill my mind and heart as I reflect upon the different craft projects we enjoyed. My sister and I spent hours making tiny elves out of felt and pipe cleaners that we would hang around the house. Before the age of eight, Mother provided ballet and tap dance lessons. We learned to cook and sew. We sculpted dough ornaments together around the kitchen table for our Christmas tree and some to give away to family and friends. In fact, a previous neighbor still has some of them dating back over forty years.

During my elementary school years, my mother paid for classical guitar instruction and included me in a neighborhood folk guitar group. She understood and encouraged me towards the performing arts because she shared the same tendencies. As a child, she too organized her neighborhood friends into audiences. Then, she sang, acted, and danced before them as they sat in rows. We both acted in the community melodrama. I played Snoopy in one performance and she was an eccentric Italian woman in another.

My sister honed in on the cooking, sewing, writing, and painting talents of our mother. Gina would post her words on our refrigerator and share deep ponderings from her journal. In contrast, I traded in those "homemaking skills" for cheerleading skirts, modern dance outfits, and yearbook and journalism classes. Together, my friends and I choreographed modern dances for school performances and created skits for school pep rallies. Nevertheless, my "homespun" creative journey continued through my teen years when I sculptured dough miniatures of my cheerleading team members.

After I turned twenty-years-old, I moved overseas to attend an international missionary school called Youth with a Mission, which was located in The Netherlands. There I danced and acted in youth performing arts teams. After marrying and having children,

I passed on my mother's gift to my own children, teaching arts and crafts around the kitchen table. At this time, their father and I had moved back to the states and served as pastors of a church in Napa Valley, California. I made crafts and sold them in order to make extra money. This is when floral design captured my heart. Eventually, we moved back overseas to Amsterdam, Netherlands, when our children were only five and two and a half. Creativity continued as I began choreographing for an international youth performing arts team that our son, Josiah, danced in when he was only eight years old. I also used to help my children's Dutch teachers with artistic school projects.

One fond memory I have is attending a craft show that a fellow missionary held in her apartment in order to sell her sculptures. I vividly remember the miniature scenes she fashioned on the tops of mason jars. I was transfixed with the incredible accuracy of her designs and decided to improve my own sculpting talents.

A few years later, I found myself trying to sculpt a new life as a single mother. Newly divorced and exiled from my role as a missionary wife because of my former husband's addiction, I entered the ranks of single parenting without a solid career. In response to the financial need and our growing desire to create, my sister and I began an arts and craft business called "Heartwarmers." For the next five years, we grew a substantial clientele by designing unique spring and Christmas craft lines and selling our wares at craft fairs and home boutiques. We even hired a sales rep who took orders from stores across Southern California. Alongside this, we provided craft classes for children, which were conducted around my kitchen table. These were happy years when our children played and created with us. In fact, often customers could not tell my sculpted ornaments from our children's ornaments. The children delighted in selling their creations in order to earn some extra money.

However, when orders poured in for dozens of the same dough sculptures, sewn crafts, and wood designs, our dreams crashed into reality. The monotony of making the same thing repeatedly became laborious. We finally faced a difficult decision: either hire workers or dissolve the business. When we evaluated our profits, we realized that the business simply did not make enough money to support both of us. After we decided to dissolve our business, my sister and I dove into long, difficult college years in order to become teachers. Education seemed the logical choice since we were both good with children, and the demand for teachers at that time guaranteed the solid careers we sought.

This decision required five years of intense study, financial support from my parents, student grants and loans, and several side jobs. Later, I needed to fund my two children's university educations. Sadly, very little creativity occurred during this season of my life. I was raising two children as a single parent while attending classes and studying. These demands extracted every ounce of energy from my mind, soul, and body. I also had to work several part-time jobs in order to supplement our income. Financial survival took precedence over creativity for a long time.

Once I became a teacher, the growing number of children entering my fifth grade classes reading far below grade level deeply troubled me. Often over 30% could only read from primer to third grade level. During these years, the desire to start an after-school literacy lab began to grow in my heart. However, the only available program was a homework lab with twenty students to one teacher, a ratio I knew would never facilitate learning.

During the next six months, a series of events unfolded that changed my life course from elementary to middle school teaching. I had a vivid dream in which two middle school students came to me saying, "So many of us are getting through to middle school without being able to read. Can you come and help us?" Within six months, I had relocated to Endeavour Middle School where I would work for many years as a literacy teacher. Moving to Endeavour to pursue my passion for teaching reading was not the only joy I experienced during this time. I also enjoyed collaborating with the district team who planned this innovative pilot school.

The honeymoon of working in a new school filled with exciting opportunities was exhilarating during that first year. The staff's sense of purpose and destiny transcended all differences. We poured our time and talents into a school that fulfilled our dreams of a new model for teaching and learning. I was riding this wave of "school reformer" when my fantasies crashed upon the rocks of reality. I assumed nothing separated me from the shores of making a difference. Then the nightmare began.

I never saw it coming, nor to this day do I have an accurate perception of what truly occurred. One day I entered the teachers' workroom and I could feel the tension in the air. Towards the end of the year the tension grew intolerable. I could not walk into the teachers' lounge without seeing downcast eyes. Weeks went by before one honest soul told me why some people were so angry with me. They felt I had taken too much praise for the school's emerging acclaim, and that I had failed to acknowledge their efforts publicly.

Finally, another colleague confronted me about my lack of professionalism and helped me to see how I had taken too much of the attention and accolades. While this helped me realize the "one woman show" mentality had to stop, it did not improve my relationships with colleagues. I bowed out of all leadership positions and decided to concentrate on my classroom alone. The only responsibility I maintained was co-directing the Endeavour Middle School Performing Arts Group with my daughter Andy. We had just completed our first play, which was a joy to students and parents alike.

I vividly remember when I decided to carve a new life. After the school year ended, I spent the summer gardening and crying out my pent up hurt and anger. I struggled to find the strength to return to work. If I had not needed my job financially, I would never have set foot on the campus again. That summer was definitely the pivotal point in my destiny shift.

The experience helped me to understand that a blunder can become a signpost redirecting me toward a path more suitable to my true desires. It was a turning point in beginning a new life outside of public education; a path running parallel but free from career constraints. I am all the better for having had the experience and would never change one painful step, and I discovered that a creative life awaited that could only come about due to disappointments.

While I expressed my creativity in the classroom whenever possible, I found myself longing to return to creativity of my own. At my sister's suggestion, I began reading books by Julia Cameron that provided instruction in practical tools for increasing creativity and writing productivity. *The Artists Way* and *The Right to Write* were the first of many books that inspired me and gave me insights into my unique personality. The idea to publish a book about creativity that would integrate my own personal experiences percolated inside and new thoughts began to form.

Creativity is a continual rebirth. Every inspired moment rejuvenates me—whether a new creation results from it or not. However, a fresh project truly invigorates my soul. For us inspirational types, combining our art, writing, photography, etc. touches our spirits as well. When "what we believe" transforms into visual forms, the belief becomes a little more personal, meaningful, and real. I, for one, can attest to times when a keener awareness of The One who breathes life into human form resulted in a humble gratefulness and worshipful presence.

On a personal note, creative seasons have ushered in emotional, mental, and spiritual healing. Failed relationships often form dark, despairing places within any soul. Writing has provided a way to express my grief. Poetry enables me to identify, wrestle with, and release pain lodged deeply within. Gardening has provided a satisfying way to work out my tensions by creating beauty in the earth. The first touches of spring often come after long, dark winters of the soul. Through various art forms, we create, and write, and create some more. Perhaps the act of creating is connected to rebirth, and that's why it is so healing.

As I contemplate what I truly want to accomplish in the remaining years of my life, I admit that fame and fortune are not among the top ten. My longing is to create. I also hope that I can achieve a far greater purpose of drawing others closer to their Creator through artwork and writing. The possibility of inspiring other creative eclectics in the discovery of their own unique identities and destinies excites me. Some would say I am all over the map, not focused enough on one particular pursuit. However, I am in the creative stage of my destiny, and creative stages need to be broad in order to allow for change and flux. I'm certain that eventually my purposes will refine, but for now I will not rush this wonderful time of creating for the sheer pleasure of doing so. Many different possibilities exist. As I experiment with different writing and art forms, I sense my capacity expanding to unbelievable parameters.

In all of my creative pursuits, though, I have come to love writing the most because it is a unique gift to me, that no one can claim or own. It is my personal expression. It is about a no-holds-barred freedom to create, and I do not believe I am alone. There is a groundswell of thirsty souls crying out for creativity and many frustrated writers longing to pursue this passion.

A TENDENCY TOWARDS MULTIPLICITY

We creative types definitely have a free spirit; a child inside eager to explore. We flit and flutter from one interesting activity to the next without a care in the world until someone tells us we are "unfocused" or "scattered." It wounds our heart and erodes our confidence when a loved one winces at our latest great idea and yawns, "You make me tired." Self-doubt creeps in like the Vikings raiding northern European villages at night. We begin to think, "There must be something wrong with me!" Desires that once delighted us now seem to pull us in a dozen different directions. The following journal excerpt illustrates this tendency towards multiplicity:

> Today I want to learn eBay so I can post my leftover scarves and photo frames not sold at recent boutiques. I have not been inside my art room to create for several weeks because of company staying. There is also a recent emersion into web design classes consuming every spare minute. As a result, my book lies unedited in a computer file.

We begin to ask ourselves a series of questions in an attempt to reconcile what others clearly see as a flaw:

- What drives my inability to focus on a certain project for extended periods?
- Why do I jump from one craze to another?
- Why do I fixate on one thing and then switch to something else?
- Why do I leave a trail of unfinished projects in my path?
- Are these traits common to other innovative, artistic types?

In order to understand what it means to be a creative eclectic, we must first grapple with certain characteristics we possess. Yes, passing through phases of obsession is definitely one of them, as is the tendency to jump from one project to the next. Yet, the root cause is often that we are "wired" to want many different art forms in our lives. Although each of us differs in our personal expressions, it is helpful to realize that our tendency to favor the diverse rather than the singular is common to others as well.

Similar traits definitely thrive in every creative person in my family and among my artistic friends. We gorge ourselves on a particular project that catches our fancy at the time, regardless of whether we leave a trail of other unfinished ones strewn in our path. When we tire of it, the project becomes a bore and we long for something more. Our fractured approach to creating makes most of our close acquaintances grow tired just by watching us.

I have observed my mother function this way from the time I was a little girl. This is why my sister and I always had an abundance of art and craft supplies readily available. She loved to oil paint at one time, and then she passed on to acrylics. From acrylics, it was China painting and then pottery painting. She moved from floral designing to gardening. When sewing or needlework grew tiresome, she began making quilts. My mother always had (and still does have) many different creative obsessions. She tried her hand at writing children's poetry and humorous articles. She regularly submits persuasive writing pieces that find their way into the "Letters to the Editor" column.

My sister demonstrates these same characteristics, switching between sketching, painting, woodworking, sewing, writing, and gardening. One of her past enjoyments was scouring the web for jewelry to sell. She seems to linger in the crocheting phase for a while, and when the inspiration wanes she watches movies and reads books until the next spark of desire to create ignites.

My own two daughters definitely share that type of free spirit that passes through phases of creative obsession. Elya is an avid artist, eclectic designer, and novel writer. She tried various art forms until nesting with acrylic painting. Having passed through her giraffe, flamingo, and paisley phases, she has recently started painting butterflies. I have watched her braid tiny bracelets out of embroidery thread by the dozens before moving on to crocheting scarves. Sometimes Elya goes on scrapbooking binges, rarely emerging from her room until several albums are *almost* finished. Currently, she is writing several novels in various stages of completion.

Cartooning and choreography are two of my other daughter's obsessions. I first met Andy when her father and I began dating over ten years ago. She was sixteen at the time and requested a private dinner with me. We connected as kindred spirits and have shared our innovation ever since. In fact, she was the first reader and editor of this book. Her insights proved invaluable in preparing the manuscript for professional editing because she understands my personality type.

I love to watch Andy's impulsive jumps from one passion to the next, and often the nonsensical nature of these trends mystifies even me. She once finished performing seven dances for a public performance just in time to enroll in silk acrobat circus classes (acrobatic moves performed while suspended from a silk fabric). She is also a gifted cartoon artist. Recently, I asked her to draw sketches for some children's poetry I wrote. I received a page full of birds...only birds! She titled one page, "How old men are like birds." When she saw my puzzled expression, she sheepishly mumbled, "I don't know why, but I just have to draw birds." Her large, soft brown eyes peered back at me, her shoulders slumped in quiet resignation. Although dance has always been her mainstay, she has shifted between swing, salsa, waltz, and modern, to recent tango choreography projects.

While observing my family members, I often ask the following: What is this "wandering eye," likened to a childlike defiance, which possesses the souls of so many artistic types? I am not surprised that many projects never make it into the world of commerce. Who has the time to follow through with marketing your past work when a recent obsession has taken over residence in your heart?

I have long ago given up on completely mastering this tendency of moving from one interesting pursuit to another. Fighting this compulsion will always remain a constant. Sometimes I just go with what appeals in the moment, promising myself that I will focus tomorrow. For example, one of my present enjoyments is online web design classes. I cannot seem to get enough of creating with my new Adobe Creative Suite software. Animation ideas filter through my mind while working and sleeping. The possibility of developing a creativity website intrigued me, so I spent months learning how to use WordPress templates. Sure, I was already busy with other projects, but like the juggler at the fair, I tried to keep just one more creative ball in the air. Perhaps we creative eclectics need to learn how to laugh at ourselves a little more instead of allowing others to dampen our spirits with criticisms concerning our flightiness.

THE ARTISTIC TEMPERAMENT

Working with artists in business situations is highly challenging because "free spirits" often resist all attempts to corral them. They love to create when inspired and they dread the mundane. Securing commitment to schedules and deadlines is therefore extremely frustrating and often futile. Artists fill my family: mom, sister, two daughters, and husband. Some of them go MIA

(Missing In Action) right after expressing excitement over a new business venture I concoct. They dodge phone calls like flying bullets and my attempts to secure regular planning times slip through my fingers like sand crabs.

These are not the only artists with whom I attempt to collaborate. My best friend of thirty-eight years is a floral designer who owns a successful business called Northwest Designs. She, however, has learned to harness her free spirit in order to work in collaboration with her husband to build quite a successful business. Yet, when we dream of working on projects together, our best intentions seem swallowed up by real-life demands, and the projects never make it out of the starting gate.

Another artistic characteristic seems to be the tendency to dive wholeheartedly into an art form for a season of time until we sufficiently burn ourselves out from the obsession. Several years ago, I had the intense desire to scrapbook, so my husband bought me $500 worth of supplies. I justified the purchase, promising to make Christmas gifts for family and albums for us as well. Five albums later, I had burned myself out so completely that I never got around to making an album for us. Only recently has the desire emerged in a similar form with collage photo frames and mirrors.

Sixty crocheted scarves are nestled in plastic containers under my bed. A product of last winter's obsession and most of them need a fringe. Yet the desire has lifted, and I just cannot seem to get back into the project. Crisp fall nights beckon me ever so gently to finish; however, my current obsession is spring floral sprays and collage frames and mirrors.

In step with this creative mania, I want to build an online business. Obsession over creating a business plan drives me to migraine status. Last night, my husband shook his head and muttered, "Here she goes again. Perhaps you are pushing yourself too hard." Pacing is everything and harnessing intense tendencies is a challenge. Yet, I would not exchange my personal composition with any other, for to create is truly to live—even if it is somewhat off-balance.

ACCEPTING YOUR UNIQUE PERSONALITY

Coming to grips with your creative eclectic personality means embracing your awkward self and providing a place for creating. For me, this is my "Artist Loft." The overall room theme screams French Boudoir, with one red brick and three warm-yellow faux walls. Pictures with Parisian themes, my daughter's painting of Spanish Tango dancers, and collections from my son's travels around the world adorn the walls. The magnetic board houses unfinished sketches and colored pencil projects. Pressed and silica gel dried flowers fill plastic drawers and adorn the window in a long floral spray. It all makes me catch my breath whenever I enter.

Although I long for a neat and focused creative expression, this fantasy eludes me. Which of my diverse desires could I possibly give up in order to streamline? The menagerie of creative madness that began in childhood continues until this day. So how do you embrace your awkward self when you just do not fit into any one category of expression? I have not yet found the entire answer, but here are a few hints I have learned along the way:

1. Remind yourself that loving so much of life is not a bad thing. While others walk right by a blossoming rose, you take close-up pictures in between fragrant whiffs; with all of the death and hate in the world, who could blame you for finding and enjoying all beauty?

2. Stop fighting your fickle nature. So what if the instructional water color DVD you bought online gathers dust on the shelf?

You will feel the urge someday. If your current fascination is using filters on your photos with Photoshop for a collage project, go for it! Someday you will pick up the paintbrush once again.

3. Proactively deal with your disappointment over not having enough time to pursue all of your creative desires. Instead, take stock of wasted moments you can convert into creative times. Most eclectics get really mean and frustrated when life cramps their style. We can harvest lost minutes for our imaginations when we resist "just one more reality show," and the tendency to live vicariously through others' creative adventures.

4. Try to relax about not making any money from your exploratory projects just yet. This is difficult for me because part of my creative expression is an entrepreneurial bug, and I enjoy business ventures. Although I long ago abandoned my arts and craft business, the desire to "play store" still tantalizes me. Just yesterday, I read about a woman who developed her own jewelry line in order to pay her bills while completing a master's degree. Now she has a flourishing business. One day the possibility to market may become possible, but until then, just enjoy creating.

5. Focus on making progress instead of beating yourself up for not finishing all of your projects. If you are going to multitask in creativity, relax, and accept that each project will progress more slowly than if you had only focused on one at time. You will eventually move several projects forward, which is extremely rewarding.

6. Enjoy yourself and others as you design and explore multiple art forms. Besides, you never know where your artistic delights may spread, bringing joy to others. Recently, a young woman I had taught

rose dough sculpture contacted me online. Her mother was my best friend while we were neighbors in Amsterdam, The Netherlands. Her mother had died since I last saw the young woman (who at the time of the art lesson was a young girl). She wrote, "A part of you went to Costa Rica. I went there for a Spanish course and taught the children sculpturing roses from dough. They absolutely loved the experience." Who knows, perhaps some future sculpture might emerge from the child that Zoe taught?

7. Creativity begets creativity. Hang around with other creative souls and your imagination will grow. My foremost inspiration comes from God, whose creative ideas flow both day and night, in seclusion and in celebration. However, people impart creativity to me as well. As I spend time with my mother, daughters, or sister, we share our recent creative projects and ignite new ideas in each other. Regular outings to relish the visual products of other artists can be as simple as perusing Michaels or an outside art festival at the beach or a park. Pull up a chair, flip through a few inspirational magazines at a bookstore, and lavish yourself in ideas for an afternoon.

8. Stop beating yourself up emotionally because you are not like other artists. So what if you enjoy diverse desires instead of walking a tightrope of singular focus. You are not malformed, just multifunctional.

9. Awake every day thanking God that you are alive. Explore free-flow writing, and think about possible adventures at hand. Sure, you have to work and maintain the necessities of life, but there are also stolen moments awaiting discovery. Often my most clever ideas come from the mundane moments of living. In fact, I like to leave current projects in progress out on my art table so I can visit them when I have a moment of free time.

10. Do not give up on your unique creative bent. You may feel like a "Jack of all trades but a master of none" for years, but eventually several art forms will emerge and mature. If you shorten the process because you think you need to be like other artists, you may pass over something that suits you. Life is a marathon, not a sprint. The prize is in the process.

Perhaps the following reflection will help others like me to realize they are not alone. My creative eclectic mother still delights in art exploration well into her seventies. Maybe the apple did not fall far from the tree in her daughter. If you are out there sharing our common experience, take heart and embrace your awkward self, for artistic swans often develop from ugly ducklings of desire.

TRUSTING IN THE CREATIVE PROCESS

Trusting in the creative process is essential for peace of mind. The human mind, spirit, and soul are complex. One day, an overwhelming desire to write is present. On another, a clear image moves you to pick up a sketching pencil. Although writing has become my constant, all other artistic forms seem to ebb and flow. However, I have learned to trust in this dynamic, not forcing myself to create when uninspired.

This is perhaps one of the greatest blessings of not having to create for a living. I am thankful for a day job that pays the bills. I create for the "soul" satisfaction of doing so, no pun intended. If my artistic desires suspend in a season of drought, I rest. For me, art must emerge and cannot be manufactured or forced. When it is there, it is there and when it is not, it is not! I have read many accounts of artists who practice their art form daily, in the same way that I write daily. They have mastered their talent to the point of producing on demand and for deadlines. Although I envy their expertise, I do not have the desire to turn my art into a means of economic benefit. Perhaps if I had lived another life, enabling me to attend art school, I would feel differently about this.

Creativity is an amazing dynamic to observe. When focused on a major project, like writing a book or designing a professional development course, my desire to sketch, design floral arrangements, sculpture, or play the guitar wanes. All energy siphons into the project at hand, and I only dabble in art when I need a mental break from writing. If the artistic flow is not there, I refrain from forcing. The reverse is also true. When an envisioned piece of art longs for birth, a rumbling desire emerges that I cannot quench. Yet, this occurs far more frequently with writing.

I often look at bookmarks and coffee mugs, envisioning my own designs with quotes fashioned upon them. Producing framed art with my sketches and poetry would be a delight; however, pursuing such projects must presently acquiesce to my main objective of publishing. When it comes right down to devoting time and energy to the completion of a project, manuscripts always seem to take precedence. As a creative eclectic, I must learn to trust in my own unique process. There are plenty of "have to's" in life demanding time and attention. Creativity should not "have to" be one of them. I trust that the desire to create art will return in time.

When conflicted over my divided desires, I think about my mother, the quintessential example of a creative eclectic flowing peacefully with her creative rhythms. Her home is a spattering of past and present artistic endeavors. Visiting her reminds me of my need to relax when it comes to lifestyle creativity. Oil paintings hang on walls from her former painting period, dabbled in when I was a child. Hand-painted teapots display their beauty while perched upon shelves. In fact, I received several teapots as gifts during that time.

Her unique handcrafted items adorn all of her children's homes. Every person in the family has also received crocheted scarves and hats as gifts. These art forms have consistently managed to remain in her regular pursuits for some mysterious reason. Floral designs and sprays liven up rooms from another season of creativity. Poetry and personal essays populate her journals, and she even wrote raps for youth. Her outside gardens and patio express her love of the outdoors with floral displays pleasing to the nature lover's eye.

Over the years, I have had the privilege of observing my mother's artistic love affairs. I have noticed that she does not question the process or stomp her feet impatiently when an art form does not delight her. She flows with this life stream like a vacationer tubing down a lazy, meandering river. On a recent visit, I spied partially sewn curtains draped over the ironing board and jewelry pieces spread out over the sewing room bed. She dabbles in each, as she so desires, never worrying whether they will sell or if anyone will think her worthy of accolades. She creates because she loves to do so. Her example reminds me of what trusting in the process truly means.

Discovering Multiple Forms of Creativity

Since I finished *The Artist's Way*[1], by Julia Cameron, I have indulged in almost every form of creativity I once enjoyed from childhood until present. I have even added a few more: writing, polymer clay sculpture, floral design, crochet, scrap booking, photography, gardening, and digital design. I write that *almost* every form of creativity has resurfaced because, due to some unresolved inner resistance, my classical guitar still hides away in the closet. Nevertheless, the two worthy suitors of writing and teaching have begun to

---

1   Julia Cameron, *The Artist's Way* (New York: Jeremy P. Tarcher/Putnam, 2002).

emerge as my primary passions. Although other art forms allow my inner child to play freely, writing and teaching seem to weave a fabric of delight for me. Both are evolving, yet I sense that the confusion of competing desires has slowly parted, allowing these to emerge foremost.

I enjoy writing personal experience essays from the daily reflections in my journal. My goal is also to capture a collection of creative ideas and allow them to flow naturally into a poem, prose, song, or essay. The practice Cameron calls "morning pages," has also trained my body rhythms. These early morning writing sessions seem to open the door to my spiritual relationship with God as well. Having discovered a newfound communion with my Heavenly Father, I feel released to enjoy the mystery of "holding the pen" and not feeling ashamed.

Another emerging awareness is an increased passion as a teacher. This resurgence of creativity has inspired me to bring a variety of art forms into the classroom. Inspiring students by introducing my own love of writing, sculpturing, scrap booking, and technology has released unprecedented artistic delight. A little hand-held tape recorder has proven invaluable for capturing ideas while performing other activities. Students giggle with glee while watching me dictate into it. "Mrs. Luna, it's as if you're a detective," they affectionately chide.

Yesterday, a few unfamiliar students rushed to help me with my rolling carts of scrapbook supplies, dough sculpture ingredients, technology equipment, digital camera, and video camera. As we struggled to my classroom, I heard one girl whisper to her friend, "I hope I have a creative teacher next year!"

My own students gathered in arts classes for sculpture and scrapbook lessons. Poetry flowed freely as they created pages to express their uniqueness. Interestingly, I revisited my own childhood while watching these young people at play. Although the finished product was important to some, most sculptured merely for the pleasure of making something, squishing their creation, and then reshaping an entirely different form. I learned that creating for the sheer joy of the experience, instead of the end result, is a practice I desperately need to increase in my own life.

Ironically, around that time it snowed all day for the first time in years. One girl verbalized the cry of every heart with her hands pressed against the breath-fogged window, "Please let us go outside. It's as if we are trapped in this cage and we need to break free!" I let them go outside on several occasions to romp and play. I smiled at my own memories of catching snowflakes on my tongue as a child.

While watching my students, I realized that creativity doesn't have to be a means to an end because the value is in the enjoyment. It also doesn't have to follow a progression. You can "bounce around," enjoying how one creative endeavor might eventually feed another, or even give you a break from another. In time, you might see one or two creative strands rise to the fore. It's all a rather organic, disordered, and non-linear process—and that's ok.

EXERCISE

Write about your creative history. Start with memoires as far back into childhood as you can remember and then work your way towards the present. Does any activity still call to you?

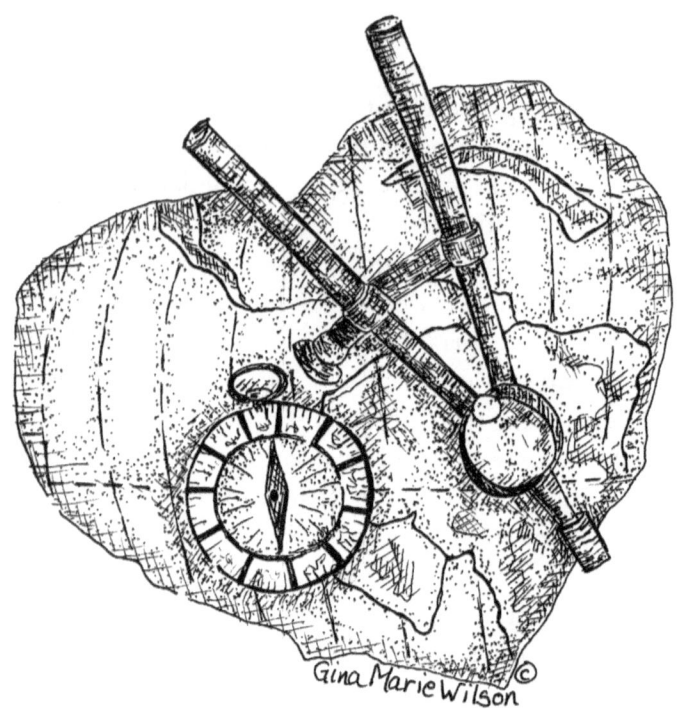

Gina Marie Wilson ©

Chapter 2

Aligning your Creative Compass

"What I am looking for is not 'out there,' it is in me."
-Helen Keller

Returning to your Creative Core

Aligning your creative compass often includes a sense of "missing" something crucial to your identity. Deeply repressed feelings claw to get out. A little girl buried long ago vaguely flashes in your mind. The need to discover who you are often begins with exploring who you were. A series of personal experiences occurred in my life that helped me to reconnect with my creativity that began in childhood. From visiting with my mother in her country home, to fashioning a clay sculpture with a garden theme, I learned how the simple pleasures of life, family, and gardens bring renewed understanding and alignment with oneself.

Today, as I spend the afternoon with my parents, I see glimpses of the little girl I used to be in the dancing eyes of my mother. As mom merrily shows me her many projects, my heart swells with gratefulness. So much of who I am has come from her.

Truly a Renaissance woman I think while watching her lift crocheted caps and scarves from her basket.

"These are for the chemotherapy patients, and these for the premature babies," she sighs. "Pink for the girls and blue for the boys."

My mother's world is so pure and simple. In it, girls still wear pink and boys blue. Women welcome homecoming husbands with bow-tied aprons, steaming hot meals, and mitted hands. Homemakers create inviting beauty with enough to share.

"Are you hungry? Do you want a sandwich?" she asks.

My Italian mother still tries to feed me.

"Look at my crystal, beaded necklaces with matching bracelets and earrings." Her eyes sparkle underneath wisps of auburn highlights as she moves to her next delight.

She croons like a mother hen admiring her brood. I glance around her arts and crafts room, snapping pictures with my digital camera. The desire to capture this place of intrigue overwhelms me, and then the reality hits. How could I have missed this? I never connected my mom with my own desire to set up an art room where I could escape and create. As far back as I could remember, my mother always had a "special room." For a few moments, I muse on the importance of us women having a special place to call our own, even if it's only a nook, a desk, or the corner of a room.

Mom and I stroll outside so she could show me her freshly tended flowerbeds filled with pink roses and crisp white daisies.

"Look at my new geranium? Isn't she beautiful? I'm amazed at how this plant flowers for the entire spring and summer season."

I glance down at the brilliant red blooms nestled next to her front door and nod in agreement. A welcome wreath with silk flowers hung above the geranium invites visitors inside.

"This was my grandma's favorite plant and it reminds me of her steadfastness and creativity," she sighs. I smile, remembering the many lessons my great-grandmother had taught my mother while she was growing up in her home.

Yes, the love of gardening is genetically predisposed in me, reflected in one of my mother's central delights. Her lifetime love of toiling in the earth resulted in me obediently hoeing rows of dirt in our family vegetable garden, pulling unwanted weeds that encroached upon our bounty, and exuberantly picking the abundant harvest with siblings shoulder to shoulder. Our family spent summer and fall weekends picking apricots, almonds, cherries, apples, peaches, plums, and pears. My parents fought with gophers and bunnies in the battlefields of abundant flower and vegetable gardens. For years they concocted carefully thought-out strategies for combating these foes single-handedly. As a child, I learned that gardening required temperance, patience, and resolve. What an apt lesson needed for successful living.

Once I noticed that my mother sometimes gardened without gloves. Puzzled, I asked, "Mom, why don't you put your gloves on? You're getting dirt under your fingernails."

Without glancing up at me, she calmly explained, "I feel closer to my Creator when my hands feel the dirt."

In that moment I loved her for this simple truth which she had shared. I also promised myself that the next time I gardened, I would take off my gloves and see whether her words were true. *Would I feel closer to God?* I mused.

When I return home I have a desire to craft this part of myself that I reconnected with during my visit with my mother; a passion for gardening that renewed my soul and faith. So I create a sculpture I name the "Weekend Gardener." I sit in front of a ball of clay with classical music dancing in the background. Nervous anticipation surges along with excitement, and yet a sort of dread pervades the air. I fear that perhaps my imagined creation will fall miserably short of what I intend, but I have exhausted every excuse for procrastinating.

The creation of my "Weekend Gardener" begins with a tottering wire fence I cover with polymer clay. I close my eyes and try to remember the garden gate I entered into our family garden through as a child. My envisioned scene is a small garden plot with a bench, trellis, and white picket fence staking off the garden's "undisturbed turf," reminiscent of my newly emerging life. *Finally, I think, this is the season for me to repose, weed out the old, and follow my God-given urges to create.*

Not only did my time with Mom inspire this creation, but also events of one summer in particular when I dove into the pool of gardening in order to cool the rage that burned inside. I still remember the feelings of devastation that resulted from relationships that had become destructive and painful. That summer, God healed my ragged soul and wounded spirit through digging in the dirt. My only solace came from the determination to create something beautiful, which others could not strip from me, or accuse me of doing for attention. What a glorious garden I created that year. Many early mornings and cool evenings found me sitting on my garden bench soaking in the pungent smells of oregano, thyme, rosemary, lavender, and chives.

How amazing that the very art form that soothed my mother's soul now comforts my own I think, as I sculpt my clay garden theme. While working the tiny garden path using brown clay, I muse over the garden improvements my husband and I made that same summer. We laid a sandstone and reddish-brown brick path that served as a daily enticement to walk the property's perimeter. A daily routine of lingering at every stopping place of my garden fueled my weary soul. When I stopped at the small plot that housed roses, jasmine, daisies, and a host of other foliage, I clipped a bouquet for our dining room table.

A modest birdbath was the central focus with a pathway of slate rocks winding through. The three stone birds perched on the rim overlooking the water reminded me to take time for personal refreshment. Melon-colored roses blossomed next to the birdbath reminding me that personal growth would come forth from thorn-riddled stems. Thorns are the rose's protection from careless intruders who try to tear the flower from the stem. It is only the careful and gentle gardener who respects the rose's guarded life and therefore receives this flower's unwilling surrender with understanding. The rose blooms for a limited time in a transplanted place. The gardener arranges roses in a vase to delight those who may seldom venture into a garden or, more importantly, to serve the gardener who utilizes this beauty for other artistic expressions.

As I continue fashioning my garden scene out of clay, my mind wanders to one of my favorite garden plots where tall crimson roses bloom. I tied the bushes to garden stakes and trimmed them to climb above the other foliage where they stand tall and proud. *Perhaps the very circumstances that tether us artistic types are necessary for us to develop,* I wonder. At the next level below, there are roses with warm hues of yellow and orange. They proudly frame pots of various shapes and sizes, housing an assortment of other flowering plants. Beside them, sweet trellised jasmine hides the shed while emitting a soothing aroma to the soul.

Next on the path are my flower barrels, each designed with a unique feature: a birdhouse, trellised sweet pea, or merry snapdragons nestled among brilliant purple lobelia. This is the area without a path, but it's so inviting that the gardener feels compelled to continue to the next plot, my grand finale! This is my garden of cultivated wonder. A light blue bench nestles under an ash tree whose deep-green foliage provides shade from the blazing summer sun. Framed between a virile rose bush to the left, with fragrant melon flowers and lilies of the valley to the right, this bench provides a resting place.

Marigolds line the perimeter and strawberry plants produce my favorite fruit. Every day last summer, I searched for their treasures and savored the sweet fruit in my mouth when I was occasionally fortunate enough to find one. Daily I canvased those strawberry plants looking for the only evidence of my fruitfulness. I savored those berries believing my life would one day prosper again.

Although I planted the vegetable garden too late in the season to produce more than a few tomatoes and red bell peppers, she was a delight. Grey stones lined the edges to create a natural barrier from the outside world. Once inside, I felt safe. My daughter, Andrea, was also enticed to sit on the bench and soak in the fragrant aromas and blazing colors. We sat side-by-side and talked about our dreams for the future.

As my thoughts return to sculpting, I anticipate the coming winter that puts my gardens to sleep, offering only crispy dead buds where vibrant flowers once bloomed. The scene in my mind is rather disturbing. During winter, the only apparent life is the rosebush standing tall and proud among the quagmire of faded glory. Yet, I am certain that the garden will sing to the souls of future flowers yet to bloom both in nature and in humanity. Nature's cycle of new life reminds me to trust when I'm tempted to despair. As I fashion my crude clay scene of "The Weekend Gardener," what I envision slowly becomes a reality before me, reminding me that the discovery of my unique identity is a process. I feel the gritty sands of fatigue form in my eyes, and so I stumble towards my bed.

I hear a sound and awaken with the anticipation of a child on Christmas morning. Creeping slowly into my new art room, I spy the "Weekend Gardener" still peacefully sleeping in a rather luxurious horizontal position on the bench with a smile adorning her face. My progress amazes me. One arm was now bent up to support her head while one rested upon a butterfly shaped book lying across her chest. As I admire my creation, I realize this piece of art embodies my desire to transform into a radiant, creative woman. I wonder, *how will my new form appear?* Even I do not know. For the cocoon of creativity enfolds me while God's artistic spirit forms a new identity foreign to what I have previously known. I can only hope that courage will roar like a lioness within my heart, as I desire to fearlessly pounce on every opportunity to create.

I imagine that the Great Artist of the universe is carefully forming my wispy wings with divine life. I see them as almost opaque and iridescent. Perhaps He will paint on them an intricate tapestry of possibility. For with His protection and nurture I can safely become the woman I am meant to be. I am grateful for the Eternal Gardener of my soul. His commitment to my process never ceases to amaze and encourage me. I dedicate the "Weekend Gardener" to myself in order to celebrate stepping out into unexplored, creative possibilities. For I am that weekend gardener whose hope is to one day be included among the host of others giving the human spirit flight.

Yes, we would all love to function from a place of strength in a protected garden plot. Unfortunately, real life is not so kind, so we must return home and create within the safe havens we design: a garden, art room, kitchen, or nook. Draw close to those you feel safe with, such as a kind family member, loving spouse, or loyal friend. Explore the idea of using your hands to create in clay the process going on in your innermost self. Take off your gardening gloves and feel the soft soil between your fingers. I've found out that my mother is right. A magical connection occurs when one plunges hands into the earth. Perhaps you, too, will discover your Weekend Gardner and your creative core.

THE WEEKEND GARDENER

The weekend gardener rests
Upon a bench of wood
While littered at her feet
Are chores of "must" and "should"

While basking in the sun
A book lies on her chest
Butterfly Tales of her becoming
Written in these times of rest

Her warm cocoon of longing
Now loosens with delight
As translucent wings unfold
And iridescently take flight

For solace found in gardens
Planted with artistic dreams
Transforms a weary soul
Into more than whom she seems

-JoDee Luna

DISCOVERING YOUR CREATIVE CODE

Returning to my core of creativity was as much a daily practice as a momentous life change. Once I determined to fuel with artistic delight, making time for it needed to follow. However, when my creative blood sugar level dips, the next most challenging discipline is remaining in "the know." By this I mean, just because I do not feel imaginative does not mean that I somehow lost the magic. Being a creative person still forms the fiber of my soul even during the dry times.

My genetic code includes parents with different creative expressions I definitely inherited. My father is a very driven, hard-working man, who is happiest when he is working, creating, or exploring. He loves carrying out projects from the idea and planning phase all the way through to completion. He has built two homes, and transformed more than one garage into a family rumpus room. He has made wooden wagons, paper towel holders, tree houses, and many other handicraft items. His tenacity to see an endeavor through to completion drives my inner motor.

In contrast, my mother is the Florence Nightingale of creative healing. She finds daily happiness in a plethora of art forms and handicrafts. These, in turn, she uses to nourish the lives of others in order to bring them joy and wholeness. For example, last year she taught two family friends to crotchet as a means of recovery from losing their beloved son/brother. Her happiness seemed to peak when she shared her talents with others. During a recent visit, she recounted the comments of women who bought her jewelry.

"I could see their joy reflected back in sparkling eyes," she sighed.

She always has a baby quilt in process for a new member of someone's family. When showing me the crocheted caps for premature babies and chemo patients she donates to the hospital, I hear her say,

"I pray for them while I make them."

Gifts from her creative storehouse given to the local shelter are standard fair, as is donating to raise funds for education through our altruistic ventures. Although my mother thoroughly enjoys creating alone, in her world, giving to others completes the cycle of artistic life.

I also possess my mother's traits in some measure. I enjoy capturing imagination into an artistic form, yet I thrill to see a spark of desire lit in someone by something I made, said, or wrote. Like my mother, I believe creativity possesses the uncanny ability to lift another's eyes towards heaven. When we give handmade gifts away, hearts fill with love and appreciation. For example, one Christmas I made personalized scrapbooks for each of the women in my family. Eyes welled with tears as torn wrapping paper revealed the photo albums within. When we teach someone a treasured talent we possess, we enhance the rest of his or her life. I have had students return years later to thank me for inspiring them to write. They express appreciation for a practice that continues to transform their lives. Passing on these gifts from God truly is the main impetus behind my desire to publish books.

However, balancing the traits I received from a hard-working father and a nurturing mother is perhaps the most difficult of skills to practice. It has, at time, driven me into sheer exhaustion. When an ambitious project looms on the horizon, it consumes my heart, mind, soul, and energy. Eventually, I collapse feeling empty due to the exertion. These seasons of burnout are not comfortable and they require a realignment of priorities once again.

So how does one continually live in a state of balance? The best I can surmise is daily practice over time. Do not be troubled by dry spells following creative productivity. Learn to accept the cycles of producing and refueling. For instance, these last few days have proven profoundly productive in terms of writing. Some mornings I could go from one piece to the next with such ease. The faucet kept pouring as I watered my many projects with new writing pieces.

Today I write from an empty place, yet this is a perfect time to practice returning to my core. Each day I pray for God to bring along whatever His heart delights for me to experience and do. Each morning I faithfully practice good habits of writing in order to start the flow. Each day, I accept that creativity has a natural ebb and flow, so I will not always stand on mountain peaks of artistic delight nor wander in deserts of discouragement and despair.

During dry times, I try to remember that one's imagination eventually refuels. The creative urges will reemerge. Perhaps in the meantime, during the wait time or gap, I must rediscover other sideline interests. For me, just for today, I will go into the closet and pull out my classical guitar from its dusty case. I will tune her up and plunk out the chords to one of the new songs dancing through my brain. Perhaps I will explore the regeneration of my worn out soul through playing some of the old songs I have almost forgotten. Returning to my core allows gifting to ebb and flow, discovering the new while revisiting the old. It also means regularly returning to this truth: I am an artistic person and therefore, I will create once again.

REDEEMING THE ARTIST

The human heart longs for the life-giving artistry that is an expression of the majesty of the Creator. While religious bookstores abound with books about living the life of faith, I long for books that help people to explore their God-given creativity. What could occur if people of faith embraced a culture of creativity?

Ours is a 21st century world, prolific with visual and performing arts, rapid technological advancements, and unprecedented online social networking opportunities. Renowned author, Daniel Pink, features these unprecedented changes in his book *A Whole New Mind: Why Right-Brainers Will Rule the Future*[2]. Pink charts the rise of right-brain thinking in modern economies and describes the six abilities

---

2   Pink, Daniel, *A Whole New Mind: Why Right-Brainers Will Rule the Future* (New York: Riverhead Books, 2005).

individuals and organizations must master in an outsourced, automated age" (http://www.danpink.com/about).

Another forerunner in the creativity movement is innovation expert Ken Robinson. Robinson helps readers to connect talents with desires in his book *The Element: How Finding Your Passion Changes Everything*[3]. My sister, Gina, has definitely made this connection Robinson describes. Gina suggests the following:

> I am convinced that creativity is like money, when we get really good at knowing what the real feels like, the counterfeit will pale in comparison. I say, let's create! Love Sis.

Yet engagement in the current wave of passion for creativity and innovation is sometimes met with hesitancy on the part of spiritual people when those filled with a love and passion for God should be leading the way. During my fifteen years in missionary work, we were encouraged to express our creativity through "outreach" arts, such as drama, worship teams, acting, dancing, or music bands. Artistic expressions such as writing, composing, gardening, cooking, decorating, painting, dancing, and designing, were hobbies rather than arts.

However, when the artistic transformation began occurring in my "post ministry" life, I found a definite shift in my thinking. Journals I once kept for processing dreams, spiritual insights, and emotional struggles began sprouting seeds of poetry, prose, essays, and stories. My identity as a believer began to include innovative

---

3   Ken Ph.D. Robinson and Lou Aronica, *The Element: How Finding your Passion Changes Everything* (New York: Viking, 2009).

expressions that healed, filled, and delighted me. Eventually, this creativity overflowed, touching those around me.

My years spent in the recovery movement taught me that I needed to care for my own mental, emotional, and spiritual health before I could truly be of service to others. During this time, an artistic identity surfaced that formed part of the essence of who I am.

I long to see more books on religious bookstore shelves that direct artistic souls in the intertwining walks of creative expression and devoted faith. God's creativity exists all around us. He empowers us to soar through life's storms and provides rainbows as proof of His promise that He will not let us drown in our tumultuous circumstances. When we return to our creative core, we acknowledge a power greater than ourselves who, as the Twelve-steps reassures, will restore us to sanity. And during the process, He smiles when we create.

THE RAINBOW'S END

Though paths be trod by better men
Who oft sound truths behold
I speak as one, a weary soul
Who found her pot of gold

Betwixt between through mounting storm
I soar on currents high
Until I reach the rainbow's end
Tis heaven when I die

—JoDee Luna

CONNECTING WITH THE CREATOR

"I believe therefore I create!"

-JoDee Luna

There is a divine aspect to creating that we inherit from a loving Father as we collaborate with Him. Just as a grandparent savors watching the emerging personalities of a grandchild, so our Heavenly Father delights in watching us come alive with innovation. Yet we live in a fast-paced world, constantly barraging us with messages, information, coercion, pressures, and pain. Remaining in a constant state of unrest erodes the sweet serenity of Spirit so reflected in God's character. The ability to quiet one's mind and heart is lost in a generation raised on constant engagement with technology. Lack of spiritual alignment strips our best efforts to be world changers with power and potential.

Creativity takes regular re-centering on what is most important in our lives. One gift of writing is that it helps us process and sort through our inner and outer worlds. Refusing to "rush" provides the brain space so necessary for reconnecting with our Creator, who is the very source of creativity. My favorite time of the day is morning when the house stills. I cherish these moments of oneness when my humanity and the Divine reach for one another. Somewhere in the process of writing God reassures me that He was there all the time. This is an important reason why I practice daily early morning writing.

This morning I awoke with the above quote in my mind, "I believe therefore I create!" Although I know of many who create without believing, for me the two are inseparable. My creating is evidence of a communion between the earthly and heavenly realms. Before falling asleep, I pray for God to visit me in the night with insights, dreams, and imaginative ideas. I pray I will be ready when he reveals His truth. Often my sleep is interrupted with insights, dreams, words, or songs. I roll over and record the content before I fall back to sleep. I have found that these gifts are lost if I lazily return to sleep.

When morning comes I rise to write freely, whispering thanks to God who gives my life purpose and meaning. I offer each word to Him, whether random venting, free flow writing, or intentional forming of my craft. However, I do follow a definite progression. My morning begins with random writing, which eventually releases mental and emotional static. From this place of peace, other writing often emerges that I can add to manuscripts.

More than at any other time in human history, the mind needs to quiet and clear of clutter. We dwellers of the Digital Age have access to technologies that can keep us continually connected with others. As a result, cell phone, computer, and television screens outshine the art of self-reflection. Contemplation requires spiritual discipline. The pen provides a practical tool for collaborating with the Divine. There had to have been times when the biblical authors cleared away worldly clamor in order to write the very book we now look to as paramount for our faith. Even Jesus retreated from the crowds into the wilderness to pray. If the very "Word of God" had to reconnect with His Father in silence, how much more do we need to withdraw?

Although I was raised into spiritual maturity on the practice of what contemporary Christians call a "morning quiet time," there is a difference between what I did then and what I do now. In the early years of faith, I tried to integrate this time of devotion; however, my quiet time riddled with pressure to perform. Our spiritual leaders instructed us to read the word and pray through our list of petitions. Quieting my mind to hear God speak was difficult at best. Moreover, I never could quite reconcile how this hour prepared me to go about my day. And if I missed this sacred time, then I felt out of sorts. Now I adhere to the practices of the Catholic monk, Brother Lawrence, who communed with God among the pots and pans of life as described in his book, *Practicing the Presence of God*. This seems more in line with what would please God.

Although I so desired this simple walk of constant communion in those early days of faith, I did not have a sufficient way to clear my human thoughts and emotions so I could sharpen my sense of the Spirit's presence or leading. I have learned from years spent in recovery from codependency that the very nature of obsessing is circular in form. The more you obsess over some person, fear, or situation, the more tormenting your thoughts become. They tend to become caught into a loop similar to when your computer keeps opening up new Internet windows faster than you can shut them down. The power of the pen is in emptying your thoughts out of your mind and onto the paper. As the negative thoughts release, God's Spirit gently fills the void with His thoughts. Human surrender rests before divine inspiration, resulting in creativity.

Writing in the early morning hours also helps me to live life with an open hand for the rest of the day. This is essential for my strong-willed personality that often skips ahead of God's intended purposes. Regularly, He must pull me out of another brier patch because I think I know the way without waiting for "The Way" to show me my next best step.

Morning writing helps me to slow down and realign; I take stock of what seems to be full of grace in my present pursuits and what dies on the vine due to obligation and human effort. That which I have felt shamed into doing becomes apparent when I write self-reflectively. During this time, I allow my honest desires to come forth, voice their concerns, and receive their due. It is in the morning that I mentally pluck the weeds from my mind and heart that, if allowed to remain, would choke out the very seeds of my dreams. I determine what must go and then seek to eliminate it from my daily life and annual goals.

Recently, I had a sense of God promising to grow seeds of creativity if I would simply care for them in the garden of my heart. I imagined the flowering plants of words turning to seed, and a breeze carrying some across the wall of my private life into the far corners of the earth. The best way I know how to care for these creative seeds is to allow the Divine Gardener to pour His living water upon them. I must restrain my usual "hurry up" mode so that inner ambitions submit to morning writing reflections. If I am to be who God made me to be, then He must have daily, uninterrupted access to me.

Amazingly, morning writing hones my spiritual senses too, therefore empowering me to keep my spiritual eyes and ears open to His promptings throughout the day. Often, when I least expect it, I see a gift nestled among the thorns that I would have surely missed had I not become attuned to His workings. These miracles can be as subtle as the gleam in a student's eye when she finally begins mastering reading. Sometimes the gift is a serendipitous encounter with someone whose path crosses with mine unexpectedly, both of us in need of encouragement. Poetry may waft into my mind while teaching a rowdy class of struggling readers. I am better prepared to receive the Creator's gifts because I wrote myself into a readiness of heart, mind, and sprit before going about my day.

There is a principle at play in the way writing releases creativity. I have seen this repeatedly when I have had students write during the first few minutes of class. This practice sets a new beginning for them, often dismantling pent up anger and emotional pain. The gift of creativity begins to flow and they often return to class the next day with an array of treasures to share, from poetry to stories, artwork to music. If this works with youth, then perhaps we adults would also benefit from the pursuit of this simple practice.

Creativity requires brain space and early mornings provide the best time for acquiring this precious commodity. Try to "free-flow write" before devotional reading. See whether your heart and mind is more open to your Creator after you dump all of your distractions.

CHANGE

"I knew he was there for me, this willowy figure
in the shadows——beckoning me to follow."
-JoDee Luna

When change is in the air, an ever so slight bending of purposes has begun. The inception is always the same. Disillusionment with what once worked runs parallel with desires for the new. Like a train rounding a bend, I come upon a place where I must decide which track to follow. Then the full realization comes; I need to embrace big changes, life changes. However, the conflict of balancing conventional living with my desire for artistic freedom often resembles the contrast of two forms of transportation: a train and a horse.

Once change affects my senses, I begin reevaluating my entire life pursuits; a cognitive dissonance begins that drives me to find balance once again. All that is resident within me seems to long for purposes grander than just surviving. Seldom do I see the change unless I step back and examine it from a wide-sweeping perspective. Once impending change becomes evident to my pondering soul and inquisitive mind, I am ready to embrace this clever master of the heart. For, throughout life, the eager seeker of God's purposes must allow the tracks of destiny to bow, flex, and turn.

In my early life, I served for fifteen years as a fulltime missionary and pastor's wife and these two roles often intermingled. Then, life required a change of economic transport. I had to leave the ministry lifestyle behind to support my two children and myself. For five years, I labored at a business, followed by a 15-year stint of school and teaching. During this time, I poured out the best of myself into service for students, schools, and district—a noble profession to be certain and done without regrets.

However, during the last several years, a slight bending began to occur. I first noticed it during the early mornings when writing consumed my soul. Then inklings of change ever so slightly teased my mind throughout the day. Now I grow more certain week-by-week that change is definitely at work. The desire to devote all that I am to my profession wanes and leaves behind only my commitment to youth. All other educational pursuits lose their luster one by one, as they find themselves taken off my list of what is important.

Now, I refrain from joining leadership teams and special committees. No longer do I spend my extra time working without pay for the furthering of a vision tossed glibly aside when another government-sponsored business comes in to reform. The lack of continuity from year to year troubles my soul and causes me to refrain from getting onboard with purposes soon to be labeled irrelevant.

As I contemplate next year's career pursuits, a voice of wisdom cautions me to be ever so selective in how I direct my time and energy. Instead of pursuing my normal course of action in pitching new professional development trainings, I will spend some time exploring what seems to be emerging in my new writing passion. I want to be very careful not to devote my time to building products I can never own.

Change befuddles the mind because the life traveler often senses the need to pull back from present pursuits before knowing what the future path will be. Like a train approaching a switch in the track, we must slow down or we will whiz past the new direction.

Often change requires storing up our personal energy and so we embrace a holding pattern as we seek new directions. We all benefit from taking time to recharge our minds, bodies, and souls. This is especially essential if our present career has extracted all of our energy and drive.

Creative change calls like the whinny of a wild stallion from the open range. The compulsion to jump off the train grows inside as you paw the floor discontentedly. The once-safe confines of present relationships or careers now feel intolerably restrictive. A longing to run free consumes you as you pace, stretching your neck towards freedom. You become more and more open to leaving your confines in order to break out into something new. However, before you jump, I offer some advice.

When you sense that it's time for change, a typical mistake is to set out impetuously or prematurely. First, develop the skills and processing tools you will need to sustain change, especially if you want to make a living from a creative endeavor.

I learned this essential truth during my years in recovery. At the beginning of the program, I was wisely counseled to refrain from making any major life changes for at least six months. The work of changing thinking patterns had to precede lifestyle alterations, and I needed to master the tools for sustaining change. Often we codependents think a geographical shift, job change, or relationship exit will solve all of our problems; however, the new, as in new thinking, new processing, and new living tools, must have time to grow and develop in one's heart and mind before outward change is attempted.

Sometimes change is initiated with a vague sense that something is just not right. You charge along at full speed as usual, but an inkling of awareness invades your mind whispering doubts about the present course. Wisdom dictates exploring these thoughts and feelings through journaling and conversing with a trusted friend.

The new direction will become evident in time, but we would never even consider it without the willingness to doubt the way we presently do things.

I have passed through many seasons of change during the course of my lifetime. When I left to become a career missionary, a life-altering course was set into motion. I've been through marriage, divorce, remarriage, the pursuit of a teaching career, and now that of a writer. Ironically, I have found that you never completely leave the old behind. The person I was before these changes was merely threshed like wheat until the important grains of my character, wisdom, and skills were separated from the chaff of wasted living.

Almost five years ago, the desire to publish became like a consuming fire. I began dismantling the wooden activities I did to support others' agendas and threw them into a blazing inferno. I do not yet know whether my emerging venture of becoming a writer will alter my present career path. I try not to think in those terms. For now, I am satisfied with merely redirecting my energy, streamlining where I can in order to have more time for writing, which brings me to the next caution about change. We often errantly perceive an emerging change as a need to alter our present course immediately. Instead, we need to first mentally pull back and take aerial snapshots of our coming year. I try to envision what I would like to do and to accomplish above all else, then I zoom into what this would be like over the course of months, weeks, and days.

For example, through my daily writing I came to realize that spending weekends grading meaningless assignments had to stop. Change for me meant that during breaks from school I needed to set aside large swaths of time for writing and digital designing.

Another helpful practice that helps me sort out major life changes is getaways. My husband and I plan mini retreats in order to invigorate our imaginations with new scenery. We found that getting out of the house and away from our work provides new perspective. With money tight, often our getaways mean a day trip somewhere.

Once we drove to the Santa Monica peer. He snapped pictures of eccentric subjects while I photographed waves crashing onto rocks and seagulls soaring in the sky. We both refueled as we collected pictures. A longer trip was to the Grand Canyon, which provided pictures I now use in digital photo stories. Yesterday's getaway included hiking the hills with my parents behind their house while snapping pictures of poppies and other wildflowers. We find that creativity refuels us as we break from our regular rituals. Distancing ourselves from our demanding careers also provides opportunities to reevaluate what we want with fresh perspective.

Getaways force me to leave behind narrow thinking. I begin to dream of pursuits outside my normal routines. These trips create desire for more travel and ideas for integrating our getaways into writings and photo-based projects. While away, we brainstorm ways to enhance our lives and even sketch a rough draft of our desires, like buying a larger home with room for a photography studio. The renewed vigor and vitality we gain from these mini-vacations sustain us when we return to the daily grind.

Knowing when to hold your dreams in clenched fists versus open hands is also essential. Often, we must fight to retain positive change or everyday life snatches the new away. At other times, our preconceived ideas of what form the change should take may prove unprofitable. I encountered this in the form of fizzled partnerships that forced me to learn skills I had originally intended to rely on the partner to handle. Through these experiences, I learned not to rely on others for what I can do for myself. Now I can look back in appreciation because unrealized partnerships forced me out of my comfort zone.

Another important lesson I have learned about change is that one must pursue it patiently and slowly. Enduring change does not happen overnight but often emerges as we take one step at a time over the course of days, weeks, and even years. Those ambitious for change must learn to master the practice of daily contentment as they savor each day with appreciation.

Change is also seasonal. Each period of life brings riches that are unobtainable during any other time. Being cognizant of this truth assures full enjoyment of the present moment. For instance, I traveled the world when young and free before the encumbrances of marriage and family. I then enjoyed my children while they grew, knowing these years would speed by, and they surely did! The empty nest transition was painful but productive in that it provided ample time for personal pursuits. When grandchildren come along, I will savor each moment, knowing how brief the pattering of tiny feet upon the kitchen floor is.

As life ushers in the amber years of aging, I will endeavor to pack as much in as humanly possible. Family becomes more precious with age, so I now visit my parents frequently and enjoy times when our relatives gather. Whenever my children can pencil me in, I make it a priority to be with them. Traveling more will surely fill my days. Recently, my best friend and I decided to make a regular rendezvous a priority.

For I do not want to languish on my deathbed full of regrets over not having enjoyed every passage of life God provided. Yes, change can be frightening and even exhilarating, but one truth is certain, we must purposefully choose those changes that possess eternal value. Life is far too short to allow our purposes to wallow in ineffective living because we do not understand change or lack the tenacity for its pursuit.

> Awaken heart of mine
> And hearken to the call
> For wise ones choose to climb
> While foolish merely fall

EXERCISE

Remember these simple truths:

1) Reset your compass: Set aside time this week to break away from the ordinary and do something fun and creative.

2) Remember the rainbow: Write a short note to God thanking Him for His past faithfulness.

3) Give yourself brain space: Look for the things that clutter your mind and remove them!

4) Decide on one aspect of your life that you would like to change and draft some simple steps to do something differently.

CHAPTER 3

PRACTICING CREATIVE SELF-CARE

"To accomplish great things, we must not only act but also dream."
                                                        -Anatole France

PRIMING IMAGINATION'S PUMP

Writing upon rising is like priming the imagination's pump and a significant source of my creativity. Once the blockages of worry, anger, hurt, and resentment wash away onto the page, creative thoughts begin to flow. During a busy workweek, morning writing may only consist of processing and clearing accumulating emotional static. Often as I rise from writing in order to prepare for work, other ideas populate my mind.

I have learned to carry my journal with me throughout the house in order to capture these ideas. Sometimes I find myself mulling over a title for a writing piece I do not have time to complete just then. Jotting down these random ideas provides a springboard for later when I can sit and think. Poems also come this way. Perhaps only a line or two at first but after working the words, others follow.

Morning writing is definitely an essential part of my emotional health as well. I would engage in this practice whether I published one word or not. Lessons learned during my years in Twelve-step

Recovery groups imprinted the use of the writing tool into my psyche. For me, writing helps me to maintain the gift of serenity. Over the past fifteen years of practicing regular writing, I have learned that my mental and emotional health is of primary importance taking precedence over everything else. Only with these intact can I possibly pursue any other creative ventures.

However, morning writing provides far more than emotional health. It provides a plethora of ideas for developing into projects that come to mind throughout the day. The random nature in which ideas visit is an unexpected experience that many miss due to lack of understanding the dynamic.

I have heard of musicians and songwriters who develop interesting ways to work with words received. Sometimes an entire song awakens them and they write it down in composition form. Other times they record the tune. Sometimes songs come one line at a time. They post these in their creative space and as the days go by, they arrange these pieces until a finished product emerges. This is a method used by musician, songwriter Chris Nelson. What a brilliant idea. Often I receive songs in much the same way. I use journal pages and then a word document to write down the lyrics. I also use a hand-held tape recorder to capture the tune. As the words or sentences come, I organize them into categories so I can easily find them later.

With that said, I have also learned to view writing as an enjoyable hobby verses a mandatory job. This is an essential tool to have in your creative bag of tricks for inspiring your imagination. Processing my days is the healthy meal of living and any creative ideas emerging afterwards is the dessert. The more years I spend writing regularly, the growing smorgasbord of desserts. Lately, my problem is not having enough ideas but finding the time to fashion them into finished products. Therefore, I encourage you to try writing regularly as a way to find your artistic muse.

THE CREATIVE CONTRADICTION

*"Then God blessed the seventh day and sanctified it, because in it
He rested from all His work which God had created and made."*
Genesis 2:3

I have noticed a pattern between creating and depression. I begin
the morning with writing in order to get the artistic juices flowing and often a time of creativity ensues. Perhaps a poem flows
forth or some other piece of writing. I then work on one of my
many projects from essays and photography, to websites and col-
lages. However, after a few hours I notice a slump of depression
often follows. One would think that creating only fills up the soul,
but I have found the opposite to be true. The project seems to
drain me, leaving hollow thoughts ricocheting through my mind. If
I'm not careful to arrest them with a phone call to a friend, a walk
around my garden, or an adventurous outing, the depression settles
in for the rest of the day as an unwelcome houseguest.

Self-doubt seems to crystallize the mind like stalactites and
stalagmites with what I call "destiny despair." "I'll never publish,"
or "What am I really supposed to do with my life," are a regular
fanfare. So today, while driving to the local dairy for some milk,
I decided to ponder this "creative contradiction." The first step
in conquering its madness, I thought, was to face the fact that it
exists—although my mind still regularly argues otherwise.

Once I admitted the pattern was a daily occurrence after I
create, the next step was to seek a solution. My reasoning went
something like this: *If I'm going to pursue a lifetime of creativity, then I must
learn to master this monster of depression that snarls after the most constructive
of artistic times.* As I drove towards home simply baffled by what the
answer could be, the thought looped through my mind like a child
jumping rope, "…God created for six days and on the seventh day

He rested." WOW! What an obvious insight! If the Creator of all heaven and earth had to rest, how much more should I after a time of creative outflow? I chuckled while pulling into the driveway eager to share this wisp of Godly wisdom with my husband—the frequent recipient of my depressive bouts. A smile crept over his face as together we pondered a truth those of us with innovative bents need to heed.

With these thoughts in mind, I endeavor to keep a careful watch over my creative gas tank and recognize the depression as a good indicator that the needle is on empty. It is time to take a break and refresh my mind instead of listening to the self-defeating thoughts that pummel my self-confidence and sense of destiny. I must remind myself that many far more gifted than I have shipwrecked their lives on the jagged rocks of depression. My daughter Andrea, the English major, reminds me that other artistic minds struggled with malaise: Mark Twain was an alcoholic, Jane Austen a recluse, and Emily Dickenson suffered from depression.

Yes, I admit to suffering from these odd bouts of depression. Perhaps out of ignorance as to the intricacies of an artist's unique mental construction or lack of experience managing the accompanying moods. Therefore, I will remember to follow the example of the One whose creativity knows no bounds and yet rested on the seventh day.

A GUIDE TO EMOTIONAL HEALTH:
SURVIVING AND THRIVING

The names, faces, and circumstances may change but the principles remain the same. Life just keeps doling out one volley of adverse circumstances after another. Each seems unique and often keeps us obsessing and unproductive for days instead of pursuing our artistic outlets. This is especially true when matters of the heart are involved. A biblical proverb admonishes that "under seven things the earth quakes." One of those listed is "an unloved woman when she gets a husband." Yet a scorned lover is nothing compared to a frustrated artist. If I could add an eighth, it would be a blocked creative soul. The volcano of pent-up energy rumbles seeking any fissure through which to escape. Some challenges taunt courage and if one procrastinates pursuit, others within emotional distance become targets for unresolved fear and frustration.

"If only my husband was more sensitive," you sigh.

"I wish I had another job that allowed more time for creating. If I was a full time writer, I know I wouldn't get depressed anymore." Yet, after a summer vacation from teaching, your dark moods roll in everyday like the morning fog at the beach.

All of us would love to save up healthy self-care for those difficult times but it does not work that way. Twelve-step Recovery stresses it is "one day at a time." Often, one moment at a time keeps you from falling over the cliff of insanity. You may even know that obsessing is a smokescreen of avoidance from discovering and pursuing what you really want out of life, but you indulge in this destructive practice anyway. Like an alcoholic savoring that forbidden drink, random distracting thoughts ricochet through your mind instead of ideas for the project you are too frightened to tackle.

Creative people have a gift (although it often feels like a curse) of sensing and expressing the heart of humanity. This tendency to feel deeply can be a conduit for artistic expression if embraced and processed. Writing, music, or art often result when we try to understand and communicate our feelings. Others who find it difficult to connect with their feelings often benefit from the creative person's ability to do so.

I have found my artist's personality emotionally survives and thrives through reflective writing and kindred relationships. When

I find myself obsessing about people or situations, I remember the lessons learned from those years of recovery. Stopping to take care of myself through processing always realigns my perspective and priorities. Turning to those people who mirror my thoughts back in order to help me discover the sources of my turmoil also helps me navigate this terrain of the heart and reinforce some truths I have learned to practice.

My daughter of a mere twenty years called me last evening, "Mom, we need to talk!"

Her words pierced my heart with fear and dread. "What's wrong?" Silence! "Are you ok?" Silence! "No, I know you're not ok so what is going on?"

Her desperate reply sent shivers down my spine.

"Mom, can you tell me what is wrong with me? Can you help me to understand myself? I have these times when I really want to do something, like recently, I decided to go to medical school and become a doctor. Then, a few weeks later, the thought repulses me, and it is the last thing I want to do! Or, I am convinced my boyfriend is the one and then I don't even want to date him. I go up and down emotionally and I can't control my emotions and I don't know why."

"Phew," I muttered. "Honey, you have an artist's personality. I know because I go through the same emotional roller coaster of manic episodes and depressive plummets. Have you been writing regularly?" I ask.

"No," she whimpers.

What follows is a rendition of my counsel that I have found to be true after a lifetime of living in an eclectic creative's skin. When you are up, you believe any ambition is possible. During these times, creativity often pours forth in a seemingly unending torrent. After the spike, unfortunately, the descent occurs. Like clockwork, you emotionally fall into a state of despair as possibility covers with clouds of negativity. Nothing seems good to you whether career, relationships, or food selection. You feel immeasurably sorry for yourself, and if society still practiced the biblical practice of sackcloth and ashes, you would tear your clothes, throw ashes on your head—a sign of grieving—and howl the loudest lament possible.

"Darling, I know you don't want to hear me say this again but you need to begin some emotional conditioning. You need to practice daily writing in order to sift through your emotions and get to the bottom of what is really going on inside."

I tried to explain to her the essential nature of this practice. To use the analogy of weeding my garden, writing is like following crab grass underground through all of this nasty devil's twists and turns until you find the place where it roots. Writing allows the reflective soul to find out what is beneath the surface; not only where the negative roots originate but also the seeds of personal growth choked out by emotional weeds.

Our conversation progressed with her finally settling down and listening to my rendition of why I write for self-reflection. How often the first part of my daily writing entails a stream of emotional vomit full of complaints, foul feelings, and besetting worries. Only as I cleanse these unwelcome visitors from my soul does the next phase of writing kick in. With room to breathe, poems, prose, reflections, stories, and songs strengthen their tender stocks reaching up for fresh air and warm sunshine. These bouquets from a soulful garden would not stand a chance of emerging unless there was weeding. Digging up the roots takes painstaking determination in order to prevent these nasty irritants from revisiting. However, the ability to maintain focus on nurturing my creativity instead of the emotional weeds often requires other essential tools. In order to emotionally survive and thrive, I need open, honest, and trustworthy relationships.

Having other people you implicitly trust provides those who remind you that the source of your current problem may just be a lack of self-discovery. I tried to explain to my daughter that although her talents as an artist and writer are still emerging and developing, she must embrace this truth and learn to become a self-reflective soul. Only as she writes and sorts through what are often only smoke and mirrors hiding the true problem, will she discover her identity and destiny.

"Sweetheart, neither your lack of career direction nor your boyfriend are the source of your unhappiness. You just have not discovered the path to your destiny. Even when you do, you will have days when your heart sings and others when deep depression and despair settle."

In that moment, my other daughter's counsel to me returned to mind. Andrea, an artist/writer/dancer/English major listens to my complaints and offers fresh perspective. She reminds me that part of the reason I do feel everything so intensely is because I am a writer. I am extremely thankful for the open and honest relationships I have with my daughters and the other women in our family. We form a support group for venting our obsessions while looking past them to see what creative challenges we fear.

THE THREE R'S OF LIVING

"I wake up early in the morning and cry out.
I hope in your word.
I stay awake all night
so I can think about your promises."
-*Psalm 119: 147-148*

I have an increasing desire to withdraw from the "Hell bent for leather" track I often live on and draw away for more times of devotion and contemplation. For as I navigate these middle-aged years, I realize more than ever how limited my days on earth are. A life worth living must align with my Creator who directs paths if given the chance. I have found these three R's quite helpful in practically walking out my faith and life purposes:

Reevaluate:
Rising early to quiet my mind, write in my journal, pray earnestly, and read devotionally proves essential time for reconnecting to my Creator and to "me." For we live in an information age bombarding the mind and emotions with constant messages. Advertisements, news, emails, etc., continually try to sell us on some desirable emotion, essential attitude, persuasive action, or pricy possession. God will not compete with the confusion typifying modern society. His still, small voice whispers in the night and draws us into quiet times of contemplation during the day.

I begin each morning with a few minutes of stretching to limber muscles and reflect upon any dreams from the night before. Next, I free flow write in my journal emptying any soulful worries, complaints, and fears in order to clear the distractions prohibiting communication with God. My prayers often fill with distorted perspectives pouring out through my pen. I allow myself the luxury of whining, raging, or just plain rambling.

Eventually the flow of another point of view emerges. Often scriptures come to mind and a time of devotional reading ensues. Sometimes my writing continues with poetry and prose flowing forth. I find that reconnecting with a loving father who longs for involvement in my life often results in creativity manifesting throughout the day. I find it helpful to keep a small pad in my purse for jotting down ideas.

Rejuvenate:

Taking regular times for relaxation brings peace to my wrestling mind, although this is the most difficult for me to implement. I sheepishly admit to being a type "A" personality through and through. Relaxing activities I enjoy are as simple as taking a walk around my yard through the various gardens created by my husband and me. Stopping to smell fragrant roses or picking ripe strawberries and cherry tomatoes clears my mind and splashes my heart with joy. My mother raised her children with the philosophy that keeping one's hands in the earth connects us with the Creator. In addition, spring and summer seasons provide many opportunities for planting and weeding.

Although I regularly frequent the gym, it is not a relaxing activity for me. I like to take daily thirty-minute walks around our neighborhood admiring the front yard gardens of other creative souls while exercising my body. Another delightful activity is walking through the garden sections of local stores often not buying anything but just admiring the beauty. My sister and I love to float in her pool and process our thoughts or take periodic one-day retreats to the beach with a bag full of books and magazines. Wriggling our toes in warm sand, savoring the salty air, and strolling through shallow waters provides wonders for our weary souls. Other delightful retreats enjoyed are trips to any place with pine trees I can admire and little gift shops to peruse. Another longing I have is to retrace our honeymoon by taking a trip to the picturesque Yosemite National Park for spontaneous photo shoots or perusing the local artists' galleries in the quaint town of Oakhurst, California.

Redirect:

The act of redirecting takes moment-by-moment adherence to the new purposes or retrieved plans I decide most important. However, I find I need flexibility in order to accommodate unexpected shifts in direction that I often needed as well. Each day presents endless possibilities, and I must harness my impulsive nature long enough to send up a quick prayer for wisdom before I jump in with both feet. However, my curious side usually wins over rational thinking because I so fear missing an opportunity. Taking little bird walks eventually leads me to my "next-best-step." For I must daily remind myself that God is powerful enough to eventually get through to me or bring about something usable from my endless mistakes.

CLEANING OUT AND ORGANIZING

In order to discover and live one's unique destiny, at various seasons of our artistic journey a thorough cleaning out and organizing is in order. We cannot make room for the new when our coffers of mind and closet bulge with useless clutter. In fact, the desire to purge possessions often proceeds seasons of new growth and expansion. Doing these tedious tasks will provide another invaluable support system for growing and sustaining creativity. For when one anticipates innovation, systems for separating and storing will help the creative person find and utilize fresh resources and expand new talents.

For the artistic soul, eliminating belongings and organizing content can be quite challenging. Our minds do not often favor neatly lined rows, cleaned out drawers, and clutter-free rooms. These admirable accomplishments necessitate ongoing linear processes of which we sorely lack.

I also live with a very organized husband who is fortunate to favor both the free flowing artistic and neatly ordered parts of his brain. I observe his "upkeep" chores that include cleaning out and reorganizing sections of his closet, drawers, office, garage, shed, and yard regularly. He rarely attempts the feat all at once but putters keeping the piles of unwanted paraphernalia to a minimum. I, on the other hand, tend to keep stacking and packing until the original surface area completely disappears not emerging until the next spring-cleaning.

Yes, we live in a material world inundated with junk mail and spam emails. Just keeping up with the constant flow of papers coming our way can exhaust and derail our creative attempts. Telemarketers often interrupt peaceful evenings with mind-trapping messages blaring over answer phones, and we spend large amounts of time sorting through mental barrages accompanying commercial breaks. These do not even begin to account for the sifting and sorting needed in one's career. Who can argue that we navigate in an information age that requires specialized tools for extracting the essential from the nonessential?

My art room often becomes the catch all as I scramble to clear clutter before the weekly housecleaning service arrives. By the time a few weeks has passed, this room intended for creating is unusable due to piles of what not and unfolded clothes. I rarely value my own artistic pursuits enough to wade through the mayhem and make way for the original until the phone rings with a visit request from one of our four adult children. Then, I shift into low gear and plow through forcing myself to clean out the room once again. I always feel a sense of satisfaction when the art room is organized. Unfortunately, I often fail to keep it that way.

So just when I purposed to make one of my summer ambitions continually creating in my art room, my youngest daughter announced, "Mom, I will have to move home for the summer before leaving to work overseas!" She graduates from UCLA in June and plans to volunteer in a nonprofit Cambodian school before teaching English in Seoul, Korea for a year.

I sighed, resigned, and finally embraced the greater job needed of caring for my offspring who finally flaps her new wings of freedom before lift off to Asia. Yet, this presented another problem.

In order to make room for my precious child's return, I needed to do some major cleaning out and possession shifting. She comes with unimaginable clutter that not even I can rival. The saying my husband often teases me with fits her as well, "I don't know where you are going but I know where you have been."

She leaves a trail of her possessions throughout the house within the first ten seconds after arrival. Kicked off shoes lead to the dropped purse, followed by the crumpled sweater, all found on the floor after our hello hug. My reasoning (and deluded mind) decided that if I give her ample space in the art room, perhaps she will return her clutter there. Yet in reality, I toss it in while making my regular clean up rounds. So I began looking for places to shift my art room conglomeration.

I assessed possible storage places and honed in on the first perspective area—the garage. Normally my husband's terrain, I fought long and hard for my section—that was currently in a mess he pointed out. Without a sufficient organizational system, supplies packed in awkward array took up precious space. My preserved garden flowers were the worst culprits because I could not stack the trays without crushing their fragile forms, so I bought some plastic drawers in order to house them neatly. I have found that putting extra art supplies into cardboard boxes is disastrous. Without easy retrieval, they disappear off the fading radar in my mind. Once I had cleaned out and organized the garage section, I began shifting items from the art room to these storage drawers.

Taking the time to determine which supplies I use frequently and which I use only when an odd urge hits, helped me to decide what to put in the garage and what to put in the backyard shed. Once the garage was organized, I moved the scrapbooking supplies onto shelves. This summer's targeted art forms include this craft, so I wanted them to be accessible.

After this morning's writing, the next cleaning out project for the day is to tackle one of the two outside sheds. My husband has one for garden equipment and tools and I have part of the other, which I share with his wakeboards and boating gear. This shed is so full of junk that you cannot walk two feet into it. I finally feel the "ruthless" mindset erupting inside that's so necessary for getting rid of clutter. I have heard it said about closet cleaning that if you have not worn something for two years you should get rid of it. (In fact, I read similar advice about men).

So today, I adopt that ruthless thinking when approaching this dismal task of eliminating unused shed possessions. I will force myself to toss the mountain of twigs saved for those floral designs I never made. I will throw out the stacks of cardboard stored for creating floral arrangements in order to prevent hot glue from ruining my art table. Then I must deal with the old Christmas lights, an old boat cover, unused snowboarding boots, and a twisted awning frame. Clothing hanging in a torn wardrobe that our children left from high school will go to the Good Will so my daughter's plastic storage containers can fit in this space.

I vividly remember the time when my parents finally cleaned out their shed and announced, "Either you come and get your boxes or they'll go to the Good Will." I wonder when I will finally decide that my own children must take responsibility for theirs. Perhaps I am not ready to do this because these boxes are my only connection with their childhood, besides baby books and pictures. I guess I am a hopeless sentimentalist.

After I finish writing this piece, I will don old jeans and a sweatshirt, heartily roll up my sleeves, and toss junk into the truck bed for a trip to the dump. I will run every item through the test of "Have I used this in the last two years?" If not, out it goes! I will prepare a place on the shed shelves for housing my daughter's possessions for the year and a half she is away working in Asia.

I feel psyched up for the task. Then next week, I will make a start on my classroom cupboards, which are bulging with clutter to the point that closing them is almost impossible. Ruthlessness will no doubt rule my mind as I sort and sift preparing for next year before this year even ends. When cleaning out, my paramount objective must be to streamline what I keep.

For I firmly believe the new comes after sudden onsets of desires to throw out. This stirring to simplify first imbeds in mind and then it moves to action. The cleaning out impulse, so foreign to a creative person, is a sure indicator of change. We must purpose to ride this wave when it comes for one cannot anticipate the next appearance. (Especially when possessing an organized nature is not characteristically you!) The girlish artist inside can argue you away from a clean out and entice you to play and procrastinate instead. I have learned to take note of these shifts in purpose that herald a new season of creativity. As if a strange wind blows into my life seducing me to expand present possibilities, my response is ready for change.

As you clean out, you might also discover some long forgotten precious keepsakes that will propel your creativity forward. I came across my first journal dated back thirty years ago when I first left for Europe at the age of twenty. The worn pages came away from the binding as I carefully turned them scanning the contents. The journal chronicled my early years on the mission field, along with meeting my former husband, our marriage, and my first pregnancy. I gasped with amazement as promises written throughout the pages thirty years ago have since come true. Looking over the fruit of my labor at the day's end brought a new serenity.

Yesterday, while cleaning out my section of the garage, I came across a stack of art books I have been searching for perplexed by their mysterious disappearance. It turned out I used them to press garden flowers last spring and completely forgot they were on a shelf covered with dried flowers. Nestled in between them was an old journal. Upon opening it, I discovered it was the first morning writings from over three and a half years ago. My heart leapt at this discovery for I have wondered where this monumental journal had gone. As I read the first few lines, I knew the old would walk hand in hand with the new into a bright future: "I feel the anticipation of new beginnings pregnant inside of me. I am excited about this new journey. I anticipate the discovery of my God-given gifting."

Yes, these days of purging and systemizing take their toll on my writing and digitizing time. I only manage my usual morning writing, but I cannot type the many pieces into computer files. Yet, these pieces safely wait in various notebooks for long, leisurely summer days when I will have ample occasion. For now, taking the time to clean out clutter and install effective management systems will prove invaluable for future creative expansion. Learning to embrace these seasons of preparation is essential.

Dreams will surely come to those with eagerness of heart and expansion of soul. Whether those dreams actually materialize into tangible results often depends upon organization. Fleeting ideas captured with pen or spoken into a mini tape recorder and then typed into a computer need an organizational system for easy retrieval. Art supplies for future masterpieces must be readily accessible. The frustration of not finding your brushes, canvas, or colors squashes the fleeting desire to paint. When one has to wade through mountains of clutter, the required effort drains creative energy away. Books grow slowly, as does a talent for sketching or sculpturing if the writer or artist can find supplies and has a system for sustaining growth.

Therefore, when the urge to clean and organize descends, I suggest you put down your brush and pen and roll up your sleeves. Set aside some long days for sorting and sifting through closets, rooms, garages, and sheds. If one's priorities can be determined from possessions saved, then take an honest look at what you store in extra spaces.

CREATIVITY RUNS IN CURRENTS

For this eclectic personality, creativity runs in currents. A certain desire sweeps me along in a definite direction, and I find myself driven to create within a certain focus. When this occurs, I tend to sideline other artistic interests while the project at hand possesses soul, mind, and heart.

Currently, the endeavor is finishing my first two books for self-publishing. Morning writings spill into chapters and weekends often involve long stretches of time for adding to page counts. I pass by unfinished sketches posted on the bulletin board in my artist's loft. Mounting stacks of preserved flowers beckon for me to design but something deep inside of me resists. The guitar still calls from its case, begging me to find chords for the songs coming nightly and daily, yet the current of creativity definitely favors writing at this time.

I used to expend exorbitant amounts of mental and emotional energy trying to reconcile this tendency towards multiplicity. I also tried to force myself to find balance. However, all efforts proved useless. When I want to write, I want to write, purely and simply. When I want to sketch, I want to sketch. When summer days stretch out open and free, I explore other artistic interests.

The creative eclectic must learn that flowing within the currents of creativity means moving with emerging desires. Do not spend too much time questioning this phenomenon that occurs. We are fickle creatures who do not like pinning down to just one pursuit. Urgings strike similar to the cravings of a pregnant woman and we simply must find our way to that art form beckoning.

My two artistic daughters and I discuss this tendency that we possess. All of us agree that pressure to create robs us of the joy and impetus. Our innovative expressions must remain free in order to flow in this mysterious current pulling us along. The finished product matters not as much as enjoying the moment. Analyzing this tendency reveals a very child-like quality. Children possess an ability to delight in a creative activity without muddying the waters with adult expectations of perfection. They desire to do something and then just do it. The problem with us adults is over thinking the matter. If we could purpose to be more like children, our creativity would flow more readily.

I like to think there is a divine aspect to this mystery. Our gifts meant for bringing to others percolate to the top like an underground spring. If we slow down and pursue a lifestyle of self-reflection, these talents will naturally take us interesting places. Yet our fast-paced, information glutted culture keeps us constantly distracted by news and entertainment streaming through television and computer screens. It takes a daily practice of quieting one's mind in a secluded place in order to sift and sort through emerging desires. The practice of daily writing proves invaluable for me in order to discover the stream's flow and push my boat of artistic delight into the moving waters.

Another powerful cultural pull that can stop our creative flow is the message that only fame and fortune validate one's creative gifting. This jaded influence extols those rising to the ranks of the world's wealthy and popular. Writing to have your book climb to the bestseller list becomes the primary goal. In addition, writing what sells becomes the paramount focus for emerging writers.

This kind of thinking often disqualifies us in our own minds from pursuing artistic interests we enjoy. I question a cultural message that places such demands of performance upon ingenuity. Creating is valid and healing regardless of whether our works ever sell or make us famous. We create primarily to enjoy the gifts of our

Creator who never strives for the approval of man. The One who gives generously to those deemed inferior by our world systems models a pure path for creating. We should seek to give away generously from what we receive freely. He bestows indestructible crowns for heaven and not earthly status from others. A rose blooms in a day regardless of whether a human is present to breathe in the scent or profit from the flower's sale.

Another self-defeating temptation for the creative eclectic is to succumb to self-incrimination. Because we do not only focus on one art form, we often fail to complete lengthy projects. This tendency often leads to self-loathing. We must remind ourselves that what we lack in singleness of focus, we possess in passing on inspiration to others. For instance, if I only painted, then I would miss connecting with other multi-gifted people who love so many diverse interests. Self-acceptance is crucial for our personality types. God created each one of us unique, able to flow in different currents which best suit our personality and gifts.

The truth about creativity is it possesses an inherent ebb and flow nature. You can do all of the "priming the pump" tricks like writing out your feelings, exploring an interesting place, or taking a walk around the block, but when the faucet shuts off with dribbles signifying the end of flow, one must sit back and relax. During these "non-productive" writing times, I usually haul all of my other loves out of my art room and into the family room area where I write. Littered around me, I dig through them like a hobo rummaging through a new find. There is my light box for tracing objects into a sketch, pencils purchased in order to discover their effects, and partially read art books explored in an attempt to jump-start a former dry period. By evening's end, the family room resembles a garage sale.

LESSONS FROM THE GARDEN: PROFITABLE PRUNING

Last year I joined a Greek society for educators comprised mostly of retired teachers. The meetings, often held on Saturday midmornings, consisted mostly of reports from committees, polite conversation, and craft lessons. Although I look forward to such activities during retirement days, the sacrificing of Saturdays proved too costly for this full-time teacher and part-time writer. After honest deliberation, I decided to decline my membership informing the president through email. Her reply assertively stated that I could do both and that they needed me. I knew I had grown in healthy self-care when I did not feel a twinge of remorse or guilt about my decision. Consequently, this Saturday I am writing instead of socializing.

There are times in one's life that require pruning in order to conserve creativity for pursuing destiny. The unseasoned and immature often require their Heavenly Gardener to allow situations that force cutting off the unproductive in order to make room for the fruitful. Yet as I age, the awareness comes that it is now time for me to pick up the pruning shears and lop off some inefficient activities and harmful relationships. The good always rivals the best. My new stems quickly multiply crowding limited moments and sucking finite energy. Not only do too many new shoots hinder one's creativity, but also difficult relationships keep one mentally and emotionally fatigued.

Recently I read a feature article by Lee Reich in the magazine, *Gardening Basics*, called "Pruning 101[4]." As I read this article, the life applications jumped off the page. The information marveled not only for personal garden improvement but also for healthy life continuance.

---

4   Lee Reich, "Pruning 101," *Gardening Basics* March 2009.

The article reminded me of my youthful years when I grew up with a mother who was an ardent gardener. Every year, she wrestled with her pruning sheers until she snipped and tamed her unruly rose bushes. I remember her advice when it is time to prune my own plants. Life applications come to mind, and I can draw analogies from her insights. What I've learned about gardening from her provides understanding as to former choices I've made, current decisions I'm in the process of making, and sound wisdom for future direction.

Mom always instructed me to leave three main branches. She explained that this created a balanced shape that would support new flowering branches: "Too many branches in too tight of an area would become tangled and difficult to manage. A healthy rose bush needs room to breath, so to speak."

Often my most unproductive seasons come from pursuing too many activities that distract me from my essential life purposes. I allow another's guilt and shame messages to dictate my decisions. Taking on unwanted obligatory pursuits begins to rub against productivity causing a chafing and wounding that distracts me from what I love the most. Eventually, my priorities become diseased and pest infested with "have to's" that prove unfruitful.

As this awareness integrates into one's life, the season for pruning takes precedence. Looking for those unproductive and unfruitful activities that make you groan when you consider them is not always pleasant because you have to say no to others. If you do not prune your activities, those unnecessary obligations will rub up against your best talents causing open wounds. Often eliminating them will require sacrificing some valid productivity. Nevertheless, we must be willing to sacrifice some of the good in order to allow for the best. Not only must we lop off older, unproductive branches, but also thin those new activities (stems) to minimize the demands on our limited time and energy. Here is a handy gardening tip from my mother in terms of pruning these away:

> Make sure to trim off those sucker branches that draw nutrients from the bush but do not produce blooms. Also snip off dead roses so the plant does not pour energy into forming rose hips. This will make your flowers bloom more profusely and frequently.

Another area of life pruning that is essential in order to maintain healthy productivity is removing others that crowd our lives with unwanted emotional or mental stress. This is especially difficult for the devoted Christian who lives with scripture mandates in mind. Did not Jesus exhort us in the Beatitudes to love our enemies and pray for those who despitefully use us? I challenge the reader to look further into the life of Christ in order to see those times when even our Lord held back, "But Jesus, on His part, was not entrusting Himself to them, for He knew all men, and because He did not need anyone to testify concerning man, for He Himself knew what was in man" (John 2: 24-25). He also maintained close relationships with only three disciples and extended his sphere of mentoring to only twelve. Those bent on thwarting His divine calling vocally rebuked and physically resisted.

As a former missionary for seven and a half years and a pastor's wife for an additional seven and a half years, I know all too intimately this struggle to live as an authentic believer in the midst of constant pressures to love without measure. I often mistakenly allowed my life and ministry to be crowded with people who rubbed against me to the point of causing wounds that eventually became so infected I was rendered ineffective. The pressure to become other peoples' answer for their pain and dysfunction crushed my youthful spirit and thwarted my personal interests. From these experiences, I learned to prune people from my life who inflict constant pain and destruction with no intention of doing the hard work required for healing.

We can draw an analogy from Mom's advice in handling those overgrown branches. If you do not prune a bush of unruly shoots, wind will cause them to rub against each other and the thorns from one will slice the other. This becomes a breeding ground for parasites.

At times we need a clean cut with those wrecking havoc in our lives in order to rid ourselves of disease so we can heal. Unhealthy branches may come in the form of addictive lovers, cruel colleagues, or disloyal friends. Anyone who constantly injures us without intent to change qualifies as a sucker branch. Even Jesus had his Judas. If we do not trim them, we have a heavenly Father who will. John 15: 1-2 presents the pruning analogy to illustrate God's husbandry in our lives:

> I am the true vine, and My Father is the vinedresser. Every branch in Me that does not bear fruit, He takes away; and every branch that bears fruit, He prunes it so that it may bear more fruit.

Even as I write, I envision those unfruitful sucker branches that have recently sprouted and stretched their necks above the other flowering branches. This scripture reminded me to remove them least they drain the life out of me.

Every creative soul has suckers in life that drain time and energy. When one desires to pursue a passion, we soon see the emergence of that which competes for limited resources. Sometimes suckers are people who have not learned healthy self-care so they continually draw upon our strength of soul and spirit. We find ourselves spending countless hours helping them process their problems at the expense of writing our book or painting our picture. Often we keep them connected because they shore up our pathetic egos providing an illusion of self-importance. However, suckers never heal but only grow in strength and demand.

Deciding to carve out time for creativity in my life required sorting through my relationships in order to identify those consistently causing pain and emotional upheaval. I began to distance myself from those unhealthy relationships by creating boundaries. Addictive people do not like boundaries for they see their needs as paramount. When you begin saying no, be ready for friendship fallout, as they will interpret your boundaries as rejection. They may vacillate between anger and self-pity. Punishing through emotional withdrawal may also accompany the arsenal of tactics used to get you to recant. Those willing to allow you the space and light to bloom and grow are your true friends.

Sometimes suckers are time drainers like housework that one can hire out in order to work on projects. My husband and I reached this resolution when I proposed spending Saturdays writing instead of housecleaning. Finishing books required concentrated time and hiring out this household task freed up hours. Of course, the expenditure is a financial sacrifice that at times we groan over, but ultimately we know that this extra time propels my manuscripts forward. Time is money and creativity takes time.

Another important lesson from the garden includes how to select friendships that encourage your creativity. Personally speaking, I have found those people who resist the seduction of power, money, and influence to be trustworthy friends. This goes against my tendency to pursue those who exude power and ambition. Perhaps this is because I have always sought in others what was lacking in me. As I trained myself to set and accomplish goals, the need to find tenacity in others subsided.

At times, the creative eclectic must grieve the torn off suckers and pruned stems. Making significant life changes like these proves unsettling and heartbreaking. Write about it, grieve it, and you will eventually heal, but do not wish back the branches.

EXERCISE

Identify something or someone who drains your creativity. Write down your feelings about this situation or person. Now decide on one positive step you can make to take care of yourself when encountering this activity or person.

Gina Marie Wilson©

CHAPTER 4

OVERCOMING OBSTACLES

"Long labor, difficult delivery, but offspring
with unlimited potential."

-Linda Eubanks

My decision to write daily and create regularly was only the beginning of the battle to explore and expand my creativity. Daily challenges hindered my artistic ambitions. Some were internal such as codependency struggles and besetting insecurities. Other challenges pummeled me from without, such as relational drama. Overcoming obstacles is part of being a creative eclectic. We encounter so many different challenges that threaten to stifle our exploration. We obsessively do something until we hate it for a very long time. Sometimes the desire for the art form returns; sometimes we have sufficiently killed the desire for the rest of our lives. We creative types possess a mental construction that alternately sees us working ourselves into inexplicable euphoria, followed by depression. There are emotional obstacles and relational obstacles. Sometimes our passions make us feel crazy and at other times, we are on top of the world. The following pieces address difficulties that the creative eclectic will face if he or she desires to spend more time creating and less time caught in life's "go nowhere" snares.

DEALING WITH DEPRESSION

It is not uncommon for depression to precede those moments in our lives when we feel we are really walking in the gifts we were given. We grow weary from trying to fit our talents together, like puzzle pieces we repeatedly turn while we look for just the right fit. During a recent bout with the blues, I sent my best friend one of my "dark nights of the soul" writings. The reflection described clouded vision and hopeless thoughts concerning a possible writing future. Her email reply encouraged me by reaffirming that I must be on the right path because "the greatest darkness comes before the dawn." I clung to her words and continued to write.

Depression often contains seeds of self-pity, which result from isolation. I bemoan not hearing from close friends when writing becomes difficult. During these times, it is essential for me to remember that I chose this season of seclusion in order to work on manuscripts and develop the creative person I long to be.

I also remember what I learned during my years in Twelve-step recovery in terms of having an extensive emotional support system. We co-dependents relied upon our access to a telephone list with people we could call to share our frustrations and fears. When our obsessive thoughts began tormenting, we turned to others who could relate.

Even though I choose to be alone so I can write, I find that depression signals my need for breaks. Those feelings of gloom indicate my need to change focus by driving somewhere that inspires me. Sometimes I even stroll through the garden sections of stores looking for flowers to smell. I drink in their beauty and feel alive again.

Another helpful activity that breaks my blues is a quick trip to an arts and crafts store. Just milling through the isles, along with other artistic people, seems to boost my resolve to return home once again. When all else fails, I call a friend or family member and vent about my morose mood.

Even as I write these words, I feel my depression finally breaking, allowing my hope to shine through the dark, stormy clouds of doubt. The creativity website I am working on is a large part of my purpose as a writer and artisan. In a world riddled with despair and disbelief, I envision this site becoming a beacon of hope for other creative souls. I will direct my heart's creative stream around those boulders of insecurities in order for the content to evolve.

I try to remind myself that my gloriously uninterrupted vacation days provide ample time for writing and creating. The beginning of the summer in which I am writing this piece marks my fiftieth birthday and "Year of Jubilee" when financial burdens finally lift. My daughter, Elya, will graduate from UCLA and move overseas to teach English in Korea for a year. This will herald an era of freedom from financial obligations incurred due to raising a family and paying college tuitions.

When my depression abates, I imagine how satisfying it would be to inspire other people creatively. This at times seems like a heady ambition, but then I think "What if?" What if following this internal drumbeat is actually a part of using my talents in purposeful ways? Could others who wait along the path of my life be in need of a word of encouragement? Perhaps an artistic idea could inspire them to get through their dreary day. Could others possess latent gifts that have fallen asleep after eating depression's poisonous apple? Maybe I did hear heaven speak to light the fires of other souls that are now only dimly burning wicks. For this I live, I write, I create.

In order to discover God's will, the seeker must boldly move towards the vision as it spontaneously appears and systematically builds through concerted efforts. Accepting possible error in our ways is a given, for we only see as somewhat blind adventurers.

We can never know for sure whether a certain way is the right choice until we glance back over the shoulder of experience. Then, we see creative seedlings sprouting into gardens of delight behind our tentative steps. All forward vision seems uncertain at best; however, we choose to believe in a God whose purposeful design guarantees that we will not entirely miss His path. He is quite able to create positive results from past mistakes if the seeker accepts a lifestyle of self-reflection and new direction.

Depression can also result from fearing to explore a new artistic talent we feel drawn to do. Recently, my daughter, Andy, and I discussed facing our fears when our tendency to follow random creative inclinations occurs. Upon first revelation, we often shirk at the seemingly ridiculous nature of our ideas. For example, I shared some of the songs for a youth musical that are coming to me both night and day. As I sang and described the stage scenes I envisioned, she began to see the choreography. However, since she lacks a musical background, this aspect of the project intimidated her. I know my musical experience is quite limited, but I do have friends who are composers. I have also researched software that aids the inexperienced musician with digital instruments and composition. Perhaps this musical will never materialize into any public expression, but I must create, for the songs bring me immense joy and new life.

Sometimes we suffer from depression because we feel the pressure to create only for material gain versus for the sheer pleasure, or we think we are just "wasting time" on the artistic stuff. Yet by denying that creative part of our psyche we plunge ourselves into depression. We don't just want to create. We NEED to.

Another source of depression for us creative eclectics is spreading ourselves too thin. Andy and I also talked about our tendency to "want it all" when it comes to exploration and expression. Unable to do it all, we turn our disappointment and anger in on ourselves. We grow annoyed with our inability to master all of the different art forms we try. When I shared this insight with Andy, she exclaimed wide-eyed, "I can't help myself."

"I understand." My reply nestled next to hers like two kindred spirits warmed by creativity's fire. We are hopelessly in love with so many different forms of artistic expression that finished products prove a rare commodity. Therefore, we must live with our disappointment and keep wary of the depression that accompanies incompletion.

"I stopped fighting it," I admitted.

"Me too," she returned with a sigh.

This is just the way we are, the way God created us to be. I know there must be many other creative souls who thrive on multiple artistic expressions to the detriment of truly excelling in one pursuit. As an educator, I wonder if perhaps our creative gifts enable us teachers to navigate the creative needs of a variety of students. One thing is certain: when two or more imaginative souls share a moment of originality, heart desires ignite into a flame. We set aside all pursuits not essential for living so we can make more time to create.

As glorious as these experiences with other creative kindred spirits may be, they are often mixed with a sense of despair that blankets the optimism that accompanies creating. Doubts creep in: "What am I doing? Is my creativity really going anywhere? Did I just waste a perfectly good day trying to birth some worthless art form?" Yes, creating is very much like giving birth. The artistic soul labors to express what it has envisioned. Lack of skills can frustrate and disenchant, leaving us scorning what we made.

An impulsive, imaginative nature is also apt to focus on a new venture before the last one is finished. We can experience feelings of failure when we don't bring products through to completion. At times, I see glimpses of an intricate tapestry woven from many talents and pursuits. Other times, I only look at the snarled backside, thick with haphazard and knots.

When creative post-partum depression descends, one antidote I know to be effective is separating from the work for a brief interlude. Going for a brisk walk does wonders for the soul. I also enjoy phoning a friend or taking a break with another activity. The new creation will be okay if the artist temporarily walks away. The very act of creating drains the soul. Like a weary and worn out new mother, the soul must regenerate and renew.

Understanding this cycle of creative rebirth and post-partum depression is essential for sustaining creativity day after day. Many creative souls fear this depression because they do not fully grasp the dynamic. As a result, they run from subsequent artistic endeavors. Instead, I encourage you to take the time to understand this process in order to mature as an innovator who can deliver many gifts to the world. Reconcile your drive to explore your untapped potential. Understand your tendency to withdraw when you fall into comparing yourself with others who may have developed their skills beyond your own. Slinking back into the shadows of defeat only increases your depression.

Remind yourself, also, that you create because you dare to believe that everyone has a destiny on this earth regardless of whether his or her gift ever becomes a popular television program, tops the *New York Times* bestseller list, or makes you a lot of money. We create because we dare to believe that one day our destiny will take us to places we never dreamed possible. God gave you creative gifts to share with others—they have the potential to be a blessing. Knowing this is not only encouraging, but also a wonderful antidote for dealing with depression.

HAT TRICK

Today's modern woman wears multiple hats. Trying to be so many things to so many people can leave us with little time for our own creative projects. Often we have our home hat. If we are married with children of any ages, our maternal broad brim extends far over our responsible shoulders. For those of us suspended between the "ultimate mother role" of the 1950s and the liberated women of today (mid-lifers), switching hats exhausts us.

My best friend called me recently, all churned up while driving in her car. She had temporarily "escaped" the family and needed to vent. Barbie is one of the unique hat trick artists who had a late-in-life baby. At fifty-years old, she switches between being a wife and devoted mother of a five-year-old, along with two grown up children. She also owns and operates a large floral business. Her mental and emotional fatigue filled her tearful complaints. As she rambled I could not help thinking, *How on earth does she do all of this and stay sane?* Practically speaking, how do women these days pull it off? What possible advice can I pass on to this desperate hat trick artist of the impossible switch-a-rue?

Even though I luxuriate in my empty nest years, switching hats continues to challenge me daily. Tuesday night culminated in a school board presentation that my colleagues and I had worked on for weeks to pull together. We highlighted the high-tech literacy program we run at all of the district middle schools. My tired teacher/presenter hat drooped as I drove home with several messages buzzing my cell phone from two of my children. "Answer me," they cried.

"Mom, call me back," my daughter's insistent voice clanged.

"Mom, can I come up to get a hair cut on Sunday and bring my girlfriend?" My son requested.

Switch hats. My mom hat is quite matronly, resembling the old crisp, white nurse's cap worn during hospital rounds. This hat houses a wealth of wisdom, nurturing, and giving. My children find comfort when this hat sits proudly atop my head.

Once home, I fell onto the sofa while I changed into one of my wife hats. There's more than one wife hat. There's the friendly "going out" black hat with a side button for show. There is the "sexy hat," no more than a feather boa playfully streaming through my hair. I cannot forget the professional counselor hat when my husband needs to unload the day's trials. This brown, business-like fedora sports a feathered fishing lure tucked into a velvet ribbon as a promise of eventual vacation time. Then there is the ball cap for the times we attend some man-type sporting event.

The next day, my teacher hat signaled a morning meeting and full day of inspiring and managing sixty low-literacy students, filled with middle school spunk. There were emails to answer, teachers to talk with, and meetings to set up as I kept tightening this safari-type hat under my chin in order to keep it on. Once home, the overwhelming numbers of emails were too many to bear, so I fell asleep on the couch without even making it to my bed. During an average school day, I often feel like I am cutting underbrush in the Amazon jungle.

Here I am the next morning trying to organize myself once again. I am wearing my professional trainer hat as I scratch copious notes of all I need to do in order to prepare for a training course I will teach in a couple of weeks. This hat is more like that of an airline flight attendant, sleek and fitted. When I create a course syllabus and accompanying digital resources, I feel the air currents under my wings. This work exhilarates and yet exhausts me. However, seeing teachers develop their talents is definitely a flight worth taking.

My writer's hat grows testy if any dust settles on her. The flamboyant, floppy brim turns up on the edges and sports a peacock plume with royal blue and turquoise hues. When I wear this hat, I give myself an imaginary name as I order coffee at a café.

"What's your name?" The employee asks.

"Julia, yes, Julia Rose," I whisper in return, with a slight French accent.

Every morning she perches on my head while I write myself into the day. Like a bird of paradise, she dreams of published books taking flight to eager readers. Her brazen manner resists anyone telling her these ambitions seem heady and out of reach. She scorns any mention of the mundane while enjoying her fanciful flights of imagination.

One of my favorite hats is the artist's blood-red French beret. Quite cheeky, she angles sleekly upwards on one side while diving down on the other. When she sits sassy on top of my head, I create as if I am a Parisian painter in full view of the Eiffel Tower. A variety of art forms flow from my hands, such as digital designs, sketches, floral arrangements, or sculptures. Her presence soothes my soul and brightens my gloom. Sadly, I often neglect wearing this hat due to overcrowded schedules and unrealistic ambitions.

How typical that I forgot to mention the important hats of an authentic woman; a snug wool hat encircled with a thick fur edging, which I wear during the winters as a covering for my mind. She enables me to think through difficult situations and to solve knotty problems. She protects me from blasts of difficult relationships and testy circumstances. When icy winds of criticism bite, I turn her furry trim down over my ears. Eventually sunny spring days peel her off as my sunbonnet beckons me to the garden, where a surplus of welcoming flowers and vegetable plants await me.

As you can see, our hat tricks are complex, especially for women. Few, if any, of us master frequent and flawless switches.

Being stuck wearing any one hat for a prolonged period causes our heads to itch and our minds to sweat. There are two simple secrets to managing multiples hats. The first is to acknowledge that with all of life's trials and tribulations, switching hats is normal. Stop fighting the reality that as a modern woman you must manage diverse and complex roles.

The second secret is to carve out some alone time in order to process your priorities through journal writing. You will come to see that some hats are wearing calluses in your skull and need to come off a little more frequently. Others gather dust while waiting for you to discover them again. Even as I write, my skipper's cap calls me to schedule a time to sail off on another adventure.

SHIFTING YOUR ENERGY FROM DRAMA
TO CREATIVITY

Relational drama is a powerful drug for the artistic soul and another obstacle when it comes to creating. If you think otherwise try to refrain from commenting during those tempting conversations when others criticize someone who annoys you. People who struggle to express themselves creatively seem especially susceptible to the allure of gossip. If I had a nickel for every minute I have spent on the phone replaying previous conversations I've had with someone who upset me, I'd be a rich woman today. Overcoming this addiction to nurse personal upsets is precarious and requires far more than personal resolve. Although I'm not an expert on the subject, I have gleaned a few insights along the way as I've tried to resist this persuasive force.

So what makes human conflict so cathartic? Why does the very thing that makes us miserable draw us so? The first step in detaching from drama addiction is identifying it as a problem in your life. Some people gobble up the misery that comes from relational drama. A few years ago, my younger daughter, the writer, expressed an insightful sentiment when asked why she remained in an unfulfilling relationship for so long. "I write better when I'm in pain," she said. Is this draw towards conflict a way for us to feel alive?

Perhaps the magnetic pull that trumps all rational thought comes from the desire to feel pursued. "Flattery will get you everything," could be the motto of drama lovers. Those of us who are attracted to the reputation thrashers usually can't resist the flattery dripping from their deceptive lips. We long to see ourselves in alignment with the complements we hear (even if they are overstated). However, be aware that those who speak ill of others may also speak ill of you.

Our society thrives on a voyeuristic, piranha-like mentality. Drama and intrigue sell, sucking us into other people's squabbles as our entertainment tonic. If you doubt this, pay attention to the magazines for sale as you pass through the grocery checkout line. Top sellers broadcast the misfortunes and indiscretions of others. I often wonder why we humans feel so drawn to scandal. Perhaps it spices up our boring lives or helps us to live vicariously through the expressed rage of others who expose people's failures.

Whatever the reason, engaging in relational drama begins quite young in life, especially for girls. As a middle school teacher, I regularly witness conflicts between friends and enemies. Everyday, someone is upset with someone else, and they send out their couriers with the latest emotional update or confrontation (and you thought I was talking about students). No, this behavior is not limited to middle schoolers. Often, colleagues collide with fury, causing survivor-like environments with alliances forming and crumbling over the course of a year.

Perhaps the greatest travesty of becoming embroiled in contentious battles is the waste of creative energy as people make alliances based on mistrust and betrayal. We should be investing our creative effort in a way which helps others.

Once we are convinced that no good comes from engaging in the turmoil that some delight in stirring, how can we change our patterns of participation? The first step is to recognize the times when we are most susceptible to drama. Perhaps we feel afraid of a new direction we are contemplating or a dream we would like to pursue. Maybe we are exhausted from our jobs and life's demands, and we give into our desire to indulge in a little upset with others. Each person's reasons are unique and identifiable with some practice.

I have found it extremely helpful to journal about my contentious encounters. In time, journaling shifts my thoughts away from the person or people I struggled with and instead allows me to focus on what I want to accomplish. Identifying and pursuing what you love is definitely the beginning of drama detoxification. It keeps you focused upon the only person you can change—yourself!

Enmeshing in relational drama is a toxic, emotional health wrecker. Instead of progressing personally, you are spinning your wheels or, worse, veering completely off course in the direction of another person's negative pull. Channeling your energy into your own life pursuits can drastically improve uncomfortable circumstances.

I know a little something about the allure of toxic relationships and the power they have to kill your creative spirit. I spent years in a recovery program for co-dependents because I had been married for thirteen years to someone who dealt with an addiction, and I was notorious for trying to rescue him and anyone else who "needed me." Perhaps the biggest "ah ha" moment for me was the realization that I poured my creative energy into people in crisis and unhealthy situations. Obsessing about another person's behavior came as natural to me as breathing, and I did not like to acknowledge that these unhealthy behaviors were my fix.

Admitting I was hooked on them disconcerted and disturbed me. These behaviors felt good because I felt important. However, as I recognized this, I started a retraining process that spanned years of struggle.

Eventually, I became aware of this profound truth: I needed to shift my creative energy away from unhealthy people and negative situations and into the pursuit of my passions. As I slowly began to do this, I experienced accomplishments and serenity that far exceeded my expectations. I learned how to overcome codependency after I recognized the problem and began connecting with my true self. Then I needed to establish healthy boundaries in order to resist this powerful drug of over-involvement with another.

My awareness of this tendency came about through extensive therapy, Twelve-step group attendance, sponsor input, and daily choices that finally integrated new daily practices. The process was long and challenging but redemptive in so many ways. I hope that I can shed some insight on this subject through sharing my own awareness.

The first step to break free from codependent behaviors is recognizing this is a problem in your life. I came to realize that I was a codependent when my ex-husband's addictions and my co-dependence culminated in losing my profession, marriage, and family. Until then, my family background and church culture justified unhealthy patterns that I often indulged in as "spiritual giving." I shored up my insecure ego by tending to the needs of others. I lived for solving the problem, changing the situation, or helping the friend. I truly believed others needed my infinite wisdom. It made me feel good about myself. In fact, fielding the drama of others became a fulltime job, leaving little mental, emotional, or physical energy for exploring who I was, let along discovering hidden interests. I skipped from crisis to crisis, involving relationships and career. An endless line of situations needed fixing, and I was the proud volunteer, continually taking on the next problem at the forefront. Endless dramas monopolized my time until the day came when I finally hit the wall.

Why do codependents have this compulsion to live vicariously through the lives of others? Often we grew up in families that modeled codependency. Perhaps someone close to us was out of control or demanded attention. We watched others function in codependent patterns as they tried to serve dysfunctional family members. Maybe we felt unsafe and vulnerable as children or youth. Often our self-worth waned, which resulted in becoming easy prey to controlling or abusive partners and friends. Others shrewdly manipulated us, which confused our minds. We began to believe the lie that we needed them in order to become whole. Then life spiraled out of control as this unhealthy friend, family member, or partner engaged in self-destructive behaviors.

Focusing on others keeps us from discovering who we are or what we want. We begin to believe that deep down inside, there is something inherently wrong with us. We find self-worth in serving others instead of discovering ourselves. We become void of personal goals because personal goals require skills that we often do not yet possess and are too frightened to learn. We rationalize that our obligations leave little time for pursuing something we desire. Personal goals are scary because they can result in failure. We codependents are very fearful people, often feeling like we are spinning out of control. In response, we seek to control others and their circumstances in order to provide an illusion of stability.

Avoiding personal failure does not eliminate failure in our lives. Ironically, the very failure we try to avoid ends up occurring. Trying to control the behaviors and choices of others leads to dismal results. It is impossible. The focus of our control just makes the addict sneakier, sending them underground to lie, sneak, and deceive their new "mommies" who endlessly patrol them. Don't get me wrong.

Co-dependents are wonderful people. We genuinely nurture and care for others. However, we must learn to harness this tendency to play God. If we do not set appropriate boundaries, then other people feel trapped and we feel used. In time, codependents often become angry and bitter.

Defining who you are and exploring what you want takes self-reflection, which takes time for you. In many Christian cultures this sounds selfish and ungodly and it's why so many Christian codependents never realize they have a problem. Others praise their unhealthy patterns within a system that extols service as the quintessential evidence of virtue.

Before we can shift our creative energy into our own pursuits, we must realize we have a problem, and this is difficult when we are steeped in a culture that does not see it as problematic. Yet we will never discover God's destiny for us if we continue with our diseased thinking and behaviors.

Many codependents suffer from common symptoms that I have also struggled to overcome. For example, one day we find ourselves with very little to show for our personal creative pursuits. The arts and craft supplies remain neatly packaged and shelved. The dance classes never taken or the book never published become too much to bear. An earthquake of emotion begins, building in magnitude until we finally say "enough!" Then and only then can we begin to see how desperately we need to change these patterns.

Redirecting your creative energy may begin with awareness, but only ongoing daily choices will eventually change behavior patterns. The ritual of writing my random thoughts and feelings down daily shifts my focus from others to me. When I start journaling, the first page or two often exudes codependent tendencies as I vent about the people and situations frustrating me. Then the magic kicks in and I move past these brain drains into the flow of unique ideas. This discipline began when I started keeping a recovery journal fifteen years ago. Today, my journaling has intensified as I've realized how the rigors of daily writing and reflecting propel the change process.

Also inherent in this practice is a renewed devotional life. When I stop long enough to allow God to bring awareness to mind, He is finally able to influence my thoughts because I bring myself to Him in an open and honest relationship. When we "walk in the light" with Him and then with each other, sharing our ongoing weaknesses, codependent struggles, and personal victories, true communion emerges instead of needy, angry people hiding behind serving others as a means of coping with out-of-control feelings and patterns.

I have faithfully written every morning for the past five years, very rarely breaking the routine. Scriptures often come to mind through the previous night's dreams that I record. Life themes and focuses emerge that redirect my daily goals. The results have been phenomenal. The emergence of new creative pursuits has mystified me and filled my life with new meaning and joy.

As I write even now, I know that numerous professional development trainings that I created and taught are inspiring other educators. Books I'm working on are moving toward publishing. I have even launched an educational website. I enjoy co-leading a middle school ballroom dance group with one of my daughters, I teach students arts and crafts, and I design a plethora of creative projects.

Currently, the challenge is to remain reflective in order to prioritize my many projects, but when crisis calls, I ask, "How much creative energy am I willing to expend on this?" I realize my own time limitations require me to be selective.

I must learn to let go of being God. I must embrace trust, to learn to listen and obey when I am called to serve, and to let go when I cannot fix a given situation. What a wonderful world of change! Shifting energy from relational drama towards the creative legacy I leave.

I wrote this poem during a revolutionary time of my life. I began breaking free from my role of continually serving others to explore what I wanted. This decision to defy my former life norms and do something personally beneficial was the first of many radical life choices. I decided to change something I hated about myself as a symbolic gesture of independence. What I desired finally became a reality when my sister promised to join. She knew I would never have the courage to do this alone.

May dreams take me above the din
Of squabbles over power
Contention lurking in shadows far below
Forces luring me lower

How many times proved sure to foil
Migrations moving south
Usurping force by tearing reputations down
Plucking my wings of flight

~JoDee Luna

RESISTING CODEPENDENCY IN THE WORKPLACE

As noted earlier, codependency causes us to pour our creativity in the bottomless pit of someone else's soul. We may learn to curtail these tendencies in our personal relationships, only to divert them into our careers. Our gifts lie undiscovered or atrophied while we transfer our need for affirmation and approval from a person to an organization, superior, or colleague. In my earlier more naïve years of recovery, I learned to resist the drug of grasping for personal importance by squandering my energy on the addict in my life. The concept of taking care of and developing me was foreign and took years to grasp and apply to real life situations. Years later, though, codependency continues to reemerge in forms far more difficult to identify. I must continue to make sure I do not give all of my personal creativity away to a system at the expense of fulfilling my own God-given destiny!

I have devoted the past twelve years to a career as an educator and benefited greatly from this rewarding job. I like to think that my efforts helped many of the students who passed through my classes. However, keeping this desire to help students in check is an ongoing struggle. Often I become "over-invested" in seeing a student succeed, but even that pales in comparison to pouring all of my energy into trying to see a school succeed.

If I have learned any truth from my years of recovery, it is that codependents inherently tend to find self-importance in serving others. It is our drug of choice and definitely difficult to identify because others laud our "good works." Our fragile egos feed off the praise that keeps us running in circles like rats on wheels. After all, we rationalize, isn't life about giving of oneself?

In contrast, I learned that it is only as we practice healthy self-care that we can give to others out of our abundance and not out of our need for affirmation. One can become free from attending to an addict and still manifest codependent traits toward others who are not addicts. I recognize co-dependent behaviors in myself even when I'm not tending to an addict.

Taking time for self-reflection through writing often reveals where we squander energy on someone else's vision instead of developing our own talents. Eventually, we drown in the muddy waters of depression and don't understand how we became so blinded. Our daily work becomes mundane and confining as we pass by the true desires of our hearts to grasp the drink of approval a superior or colleague offers.

Resisting the pull towards living for others can be challenging, especially in the workplace where the pressure to perform can especially sting the codependent. Even when we begin to change our habits and cultivate personal interests, it is difficult to resist the feeling that we have to explain ourselves. And yes, people who have become accustomed to the constant flow of energy and service we provide may criticize us when we stop.

But resist we must if we are to discover our gifts and why we were given them. Our talents will delight others in unimaginable ways if we finally develop our own dreams. It is a struggle to let go of an identity gleaned by years invested in an occupation. Yet with a little distance, perspective rushes in and we marvel at how we could have let work consume our entire being.

You may ask, "How do I know whether my efforts are misplaced?" To answer that, a simple diagnosis of your depression level is in order. Has your joy been replaced by thoughts of, "I have to." Does going to work create feelings of imprisonment and dread? Do you long for creative pursuits but don't have time to explore them? Has work taken on a life of its own that consumes all of your mental, emotional, and spiritual energy?

After you realize there is a problem, how do you break free from these codependent situations? Simply put, "When the pain becomes more than the pleasure you will make changes." I learned these words of wisdom from my former Twelve-step sponsor, Mary. The season when you decide to leave an unhealthy situation is much like leaving an unhealthy lover. You momentarily pull away only to feel the impact of going without your drug, and then you run back to the comfort of the familiar. Yet, eventually the familiar brings more emotional pain and disappointment. Finally, you decide to make healthy choices instead.

In order to sort through your priorities, I suggest you begin slowly by evaluating every activity you do that is not required by contract. List them one by one and ask yourself a series of questions:

1. Do I really like doing this?
2. Why am I doing this?
3. Am I trying to please or get kudos from someone?
4. Does my sense of self-importance link to this task?
5. Do I have feelings of resentment because others take me for granted?
6. If I had more time, what would I like to pursue?

After this fearless, honest inventory, decide on one activity that you will cease to do. If you have made a lengthy commitment that you cannot break, then select an activity you can let go of. Purposefully add something creative into your life in place of the discontinued activity in order to avoid filling it with serving someone else. One by one, begin to shift away from those activities where you are volunteering in order to secure the praise of others. Begin to draw a sense of identity from pursuing your own passions and interests.

Resist the temptation to return to previous behaviors even in the midst of criticism. Be cognizant that some people will dislike you changing your patterns because they have benefited from your service to them. Not all people play fair and some may just slander you in order to evoke guilt and a return to the former arrangement.

Yes, I will continue to devote myself to students in my classes but not to the extent that I fail to develop my own interests outside of my career. What wisdom and encouragement do I have to impart to students if I am bitter and spent? Kids sense new life and enthusiasm when teachers share their passions. Perhaps the greatest gift we can give to young minds is to model for them how to pursue our dreams.

FLYING SOLO

"No one will build your dreams quite like you!"

-JoDee Luna

I am a perpetual others-centered procrastinator, typically waiting for another kindred soul to join me in my latest quest before proceeding. The enjoyment of creating in tandem exhilarates me. Moreover, creative partnerships have graced some of the most productive times of my life. I simply flourish when imaginative minds brainstorm ideas together. Yet I have learned that even though collaborative creativity provides a sustaining support system, there are times when I must press on alone. My dreams would never have materialized if I had waited for someone to get onboard. One of the editors of this book, Kay Johnson, expressed these sentiments perfectly: "I am inspired by collaboration too, but I think sometimes we should also inspire each other to find our own voices."

Some of my most enjoyable memories are from the years my sister and I owned our arts and craft business, called Heartwarmers. I loved imagining, designing, producing, and marketing together. Years later, I still have people stop me in public to express thanks for the dough sculptures they display every Christmas. Their next question is, "Do you think you and your sister will ever sell crafts again?"

"Unfortunately not," I return. "Our jobs as teachers are far too demanding. Now we teach students arts and crafts."

Even though this is my staple answer, deep inside I still play around with the idea of creating and selling. "If my schedule ever opens up again and I have someone to do it with me," I rationalize.

Even though my sister and I stopped our business fourteen years ago in order to return to school, I still enjoy moments when we share our recent art projects and writing pieces. We stir each other's imaginations and sometimes even temporarily dream of future collaboration. Yet upon returning to real life, all of these conversations evaporate like mist in the path of the morning sun.

Perhaps one of the reasons I still long for creative partnerships is because new terrain is so terrifying. I had never written books, built websites, or designed digital resources before taking on any of those ventures. My insecurities about doing these things tempted me to wait for some magical person to teach me, join me, or inspire me. Eventually, the pursuit of others ended up disappointing me.

Finally, I came to the realization that I must pursue my dreams alone. This awareness did not come quickly or easily. In fact, just a few weeks ago I caught myself saying "we" when discussing my creativity website with a close friend. Yet the harsh reality remains that others simply do not see nor want the same dreams that I do; and rightly so, for we each have our unique desires and plans. Some even enjoy a lively conversation about possibilities, but when I suggest meeting, they politely exit the conversation and never bring it up again. Once again, Kay's insights provide perspective:

> A creative partnership, even though it's inspiring,
> can also be a distraction from the things that are in
> our hearts to do. I do think there are times when a
> collaboration just works, and it's awesome when it does!
> But we must be prepared to move forward alone. If you
> keep moving forward, you find, happily, that creative

partnerships happen along the way here and there. I think maybe it's that "trust" thing again.

In all actuality, my family and friends provide wonderful sounding boards for bouncing off ideas. Although they do not wish to become partners in any of my endeavors, they will listen. They also represent a fair distribution of potential readers and web viewers, and they provide invaluable suggestions. I have also found a group of writers who encourage one another online. We get together sporadically or just chat with each other over the phone. We don't have to wait for official meetings because we can email, call, or Skype each other whenever we need feedback.

A couple of my colleagues are writers, and we often share while walking down school hallways. In spite of my planning, plotting, and coercing, not one of these dear friends has ever taken my bait to work on a project together. Therefore, I have had to summon the inner resolve to go it alone. My friend Kay encouraged me to consider that perhaps their lack of interest was God's way of pushing me to move forward alone.

Flying solo in the pursuit of your dreams requires an enormous amount of determination in order to avoid giving up. I have found the most effective way to accomplish this is by riding the wind currents of what I delight in doing. Why fly into the wind with ventures you do not like? I cull out activities that do not seem a good fit for my creative goals. This often entails restructuring plans and being willing to allow some dreams to die entirely, especially those dependent upon someone else.

When I dream of expanding my projects, I ask myself whether I am willing to learn the skills needed for the venture. If the answer is a resounding yes, and the time involved is reasonable, then I consider the new activity. For instance, when I wanted my own websites, I decided to learn professional web design in order to explore optimum creative online expression. Using a template just would not satisfy. Of course, I now know there are easier ways to do this, but I was willing to gain the required skills, which now open the door to future creative web projects.

The process of writing books also demanded thorough research in order to decide between pursuing traditional publishing or self-publishing. I spent time writing down my values and goals before finally determining the best fit. As I prepare for publishing, I know I will need to utilize the expertise of the company I chose and their extensive marketing plan. I also realize I will have to market myself. This sends shivers down my spine and stirs up the compulsion to recruit once again, but this time I will fly solo, thank you!

LOST THE ART ROOM. GAINED THE ARTIST

This Sunday, I moved my university daughter out of her apartment and temporarily back home. This was the last of many college moves she and I performed, often two to three times per year. She will have to come back home for the summer in preparation for a year overseas. A series of vaccinations is on the agenda, which will require recuperation and mother's tender loving care. I must admit, a twinge of remorse swept away my fantasies of using my art room for a summer's artistic exploration, yet I cherish every moment I spend with my delight and kindred spirit. My precious daughter also helps me to remember how essential flexibility is for the creative soul. Without it, unexpected changes, such as giving up your creative space, will dismantle your inspiration.

In all fairness, my artist's loft was originally her bedroom since she was six. Over the years, we changed the motif depending upon her emerging artistic decorating desires. The last transformation stuck as together we painted one of the walls brick red with a faux finish and the other three walls the warm, yellow amber of a Tuscan sunset. The room now displays her artwork including two self-portraits in charcoal and several acrylic paintings of Latin dancers. The bright smile of my other daughter, Andrea, radiates in a picture that hangs next to a mask she sculpted. The room accommodates all three of our artistic needs as we occasionally gather to create, using the large table to host art supplies I keep stocked. Sometimes, Elya even brings friends.

"Mom, can I have these paint brushes you've never used?" seems the standard question.

Of course I give in, so overjoyed at their prolific practice of painting. Sure, I admit to a bit of grieving over the loss of my artistic space for such an extended time but our precious days together will sustain our hearts during the long months which we will be separated for.

"Mom, I want to finish my novel this summer. Let's find a cozy café and write together," she bubbles over the phone.

"You had better want to write because I plan on finishing a manuscript this summer," I return. She is low maintenance to have at home. Just give her some paintbrushes, acrylic paints, and a few canvases and she will entertain herself for hours.

This is a momentous summer for the both of us—a passage of sorts, marking her departure from university life as she cuts the last strings of dependency upon mom. I cannot imagine a year apart, so I plan to take my first overseas trip since leaving Europe fifteen years ago. It took living abroad to get my parents overseas when I was Elya's age. How interesting to experience the recycling of family history.

"You've just got to come and visit me," she pleads. "A year is a very long time!"

The news about North Korea's ruler threatening to invade, and the bombing of South Korea, disconcerts my soul because I know she will be teaching only a short distance away in Seoul. My precious daughter charges headlong into the thick of things with no concept of danger, like some wild-eyed fawn wandering from her doe into the open field during hunting season. If I think through the possible repercussions, I cannot breathe. Calming my heart through prayer seems to be the only consolation.

"Please protect her, Lord," I manage to squeak.

So in light of life changes, I surrender my art room in order to have the artist return home, even if for only a short summer. The one who inspired its creation and decoration deserves habitation rights. If all goes well, we will write side by side during the summer months, and I might even try my hand at acrylic painting. Perhaps another painter will be born. Together we will write away the hours, only occasionally interrupting with a brief request for a reading critique.

"Mom, listen to this. How does it sound?" Soon, these familiar words will break the house's silence.

Life's passages are challenging at times. I lose a daughter but gain a traveling companion. My summer art ambitions will have to alter somewhat to embrace sketching on the couch where I usually write. Yet I will kiss her cheek as she slumbers, and I will enjoy our short interlude before she permanently launches out into the world. This and other similar circumstances have taught me that giving up my creative space expands my flexibility. I'm learning to "go with the flow" as I allow life's interruptions to become a source of inspiration.

When people or circumstances temporarily invade your space, it creates a necessity to organize, often resulting in newly designed creative spaces. I have found that creativity need not stop when circumstances force us to readjust. Whether I use the kitchen table to design floral arrangements or sketch in my favorite writing spot on the couch, the passion for artistic activities never dies. Like a river tributary blocked by a mudslide or fallen tree, it merely finds another route to the sea.

EXERCISE

Find a nook, table, or room to call your artistic own. Set up a few decorative items that inspire you. Place a potential project in this creative space and ponder ideas as you pass by your work in progress.

Chapter 5

Developing Creativity

"Words dance like fairies on the chuckle of my delight.
Does the soul ever grow old or the desire to create ever cease?"
—JoDee Luna

Finding Creative Inspiration

Although the creative support of family is wonderful, what about those lone artistic souls separated from such? When isolated from creative people, one must find other sources of inspiration. I have weathered times when family was far away. Moreover, I have also felt alone when a new gift needed cultivating but no one in my circle of friends or family could relate. In both situations, I depended upon other forms of creative support that includes books, online resources, and blogging.

Over the years, I have greatly benefited from artists and writers chronicling their advice and insights in books. One can glean tremendous amounts of creative ideas and emotional support from reading books written by others in order to pass on their information and expertise. The benefits of books for supporting one's creativity are multifaceted. For example, the reader passes through the pages at his or her own pace. Scaffolding stretches out unrushed before you as you read, ponder, and implement.

Finding an author of kindred spirit is paramount for the creative eclectic. Often interests develop through the rich infusion of others recording their paths or explaining their ideas. I am a stanch supporter of this form of mentoring having greatly benefited from the practice of reading throughout my ministry, recovery, business, and educational years. The writings of others propelled my own self-realization, artistic talents, and writing passions forward. Even if the authors you feel especially drawn to express beliefs discordant with your own, you can choose what practices to integrate into your life and leave the rest behind.

Having greatly benefited from other creative authors, I felt it was my turn to toss some personal experience into the pool of writing. This decision reinforced recently during a spontaneous discussion with two eighth grade students. One is an avid poet who lit up upon hearing that I was a writer as well. She started firing questions at me concerning how to get a story in her mind onto paper. The joy in her face radiated as she found someone who understood her strange experiences of awakening with poems running through her mind. I found our interchange delightful and passed on some writing tips and artistic tricks I have learned. She asked how she could buy my future books written on developing creativity and writing. This experience reinforced the need for mentoring in my mind.

Another form of artistic support is online websites. Often creativity housed in Internet form provides quick references for finding out the "how to's" of a particular craft or art idea. Google a question and possible answers list before your eyes. The advent of the Internet includes connecting artistic people together through chat rooms and interactive blogs sites. Social networking sites also provide avenues for posting artwork, writing, and contact information. Others can leave comments to which you can respond as you enjoy this social support system.

Although providing tremendous benefits, a word of caution is in order concerning utilizing these resources. I have observed people so swept up in these forms of communication that they have little time left over for pursuing their own art forms. Hours spent online answering emails or engaging in discussions drains energy normally poured into life pursuits. Learning to manage these often novel and delightful tools takes some practice. Even with others begging me to join one of the most popular social networking sites, I have chosen to refrain until my book readies for editing and the summer stretches out before me. Former experience with online interactive sites has helped form this decision along with work colleagues complaining about the amount of Internet drama they engage in. My last stretch along the publishing path must not be interrupted lest I lose momentum.

I also find blogging to be a wonderful way to reignite my creative inspiration. The world of bloggers provides endless posts that feature creative ideas. Moreover, you truly become a part of a virtual community that exchanges ideas, advice, and support. The world of blogging has eliminated the intense feelings of loneliness I struggled with before blogging. I have met so many delightful and inspirational people that take the time to exchange information and pictures with one another.

Blogging provides a model for us creative eclectics who want to express our voice. We do not have to be famous authors with extensive speaking platforms to put our writing and artwork online. This is so essential because we live in a culture fixated on celebrity worship. Those the media deems "chosen ones" elevate above the rest. Yet how many of us can relate to the famous person who broke into the fields of the arts, entertainment, or publishing? Perhaps there is a place for simple people possessing talents and ideas to express themselves. Books featuring creativity, writing, and poetry may line shelves. Captivating memoirs may become bestsellers, but each of us has a circle of friends who knows us. Because they trust in our creative pilgrimage, they would benefit from books and blog posts we bring into the world and perhaps pass them on to others.

DREAMS

D reams are a powerful conduit of creativity. I am not an expert on the subject but merely share from a lifetime of experience. Ideas for poems, prose, essays, books, and songs found their inception through dreams. Insights into crucial decisions and future visions whispered through the night, wrestling with life purposes.

Often my dreams are a mix of unsettled thoughts and unanswered questions. At other times, they are quite random in nature and meaningless in content. Sometimes they generate from something I experienced during the day. Then there are times when wisdom visits in such an amazing way that I could not have made up the content of the dream. Most often, dreams flow with creative ideas that I wake up from during the night and in the morning. Over the years, I have learned to take diligent steps to record all of my dreams—even the seemingly absurd—because I was often surprised that their content came around again in some other message or circumstance by day. Yes, dreams can also be a gift from God for helping us humans search for and understand our creative destiny.

As far back as I can remember, I have always dreamed. In my youthful years, I experienced pleasant dreams as well as night terrors. Sleepwalking and sleep talking were also standard behavior. My sister and I shared a room so she had to learn the fine art of talking me back into my bed. She said my eyes would be open, and I would even answer her at times. She would direct me as if I was a robot following her every command. There is not enough space in one short reflection to record all of my experiences concerning dreams. This is another book in progress. However, suffice to say that creative eclectics would do well from learning a few simple tips for increasing their dreaming potential.

First, I encourage you to place a notebook, pen, and flashlight on your nightstand. If you awaken from the dream in the middle of the night, you will be tempted to roll over and fall back to sleep. However, most dreams are lost if we fail to record them when they grace our minds. When you awaken from a dream, spend a few minutes laying still allowing the dream to become clearer in your mind. Often you will find that recalling details becomes possible if you rest for a while and ponder. Then, write down whatever images and or messages were in your dream. I used to feel foolish doing this until I started to see my dreams revisit in other forms during the day. For instance, I would read a book in which the author used the same imagery as in my dream. These reoccurring experiences convinced me to refrain from judging my dream, but to record it.

Another helpful hint is creating an organizational system for your dreams. Adding a table of contents to the beginning pages of my journals helped me to reference past dreams. I also started typing those that proved significant into my computer for safekeeping. Nothing is more frustrating than trying to find a specific dream amidst piles of journals.

In time I began to see similar properties that dreams possess occur with creativity received during the day. It is as if a mental fog dissipates revealing a distinct image, message, or song. Ideas that come during waking hours are treated with the same respect and due diligence as dreams are. Stopping to write these ideas down is very important for I have found that rarely do complete forms of anything come to me during night or day. Most often, I must piece together the poem, reflection, or song over time.

This leads me to another important point. Creative people need sufficient "brain space." We need to be able to process the flow of thoughts that pass through our scattered minds. Sorting and sifting requires sufficient mental energy. What we record or ignore is not easily achieved in the midst of chaos.

ENHANCING CREATIVITY THROUGH GARDENING

My gardens are priceless in so many ways. They provide end-less enjoyment and artistic pleasure along with healthy ways to vent pent up anger. On this particular day as I write, I capture some of the magic of gardening. Nothing revitalizes my creative energy faster than strolling through my modest backyard gardens; my secret place to renew my soul. As if led by an unseen force, a much-needed mental break (after a three-hour writing session) leads me to open the backdoor. Stepping outside onto the patio splashes brisk spring air onto my face and awakens sluggish senses. As I view a beautiful array of freshly planted flowers, it instantly restores my creative longings. The desire I have to put into words how gardens delight, heal, and inspire, bubbles within like a moun-tain stream brimming with melted snow.

Every day my gardens mesmerize by displaying their unique collection of foliage. Each nook I planted for a different purpose intrigues me. My secret garden hiding in the far corner provides an abundance of strawberries, my favorite fruit since childhood. Additional tomato plants regularly yield salad toppings. Before the corner shade tree grew too expansive covering a large portion of the area, I used to harvest cucumbers, squash, cantaloupes, and herbs. Now I must search for another sunny spot.

Snug against the patio is the rose garden with brilliant blood-red blooms accented with sweet, snow-white honeysuckle. I love the wafting scents blowing to where I sit to write. Assorted flowering plants in pots adorn the ground below the Joseph's Coat roses of yellow and amber hues. Patio pots of various shapes and sizes ride in wooden wagons and flower carts. Each year I delight in arranging different plant and color combinations.

My gardens also heal! Some areas I design carefully and some I haphazardly place depending on my mood. One summer, I worked through intense feelings of hurt and anger from betrayal. The ground proved the safer of victims as I ripped a five by thirty foot section of grass up against the back wall. My disgruntled mood joined ranks with the compulsion to control, which resulted in a neat line of bushes planted at two feet intervals. I dug up the rose bushes previously growing in the grass in order to move them forward. It felt good to pierce the soil repeatedly, and my tears of frustration watered the earth.

My gardens also inspire. Often I venture into the yard in order to refresh creative juices. One can learn an abundance of lessons from connecting with the earth through gardening. If writing becomes stressful, I plop into the porch swing, turn on my fountain, and drink in the natural beauty. Every writer should consider a garden. Enjoying the fruit of your labors through this hobby will sustain when writing becomes tedious and tenuous.

I fondly remember one particularly glorious day when my daughter, Andy and I enjoyed my gardens. What a remarkable morning that was! I felt like a fat cat sunning in the window. I ventured out to buy a hazelnut latte and then walked around my garden areas, coffee in hand, admiring their beauty. Vibrant blue morning glories standing high on their trellis announced the day. The vibrant colors enticed me into a brief hypnotic trace. I counted the remaining surviving peaches on my new peach tree—three. If I can taste just one, I will feel accomplished at husbandry.

Andy had come over in the early evening to enjoy the gardens with me. We marveled at the fruit of our labor in the vegetable garden we had planted together. Her face beamed with joy as she gently drew back the blanket of leaves to reveal a cantaloupe the size of a grapefruit. I followed the cucumber vine trellised up a nearby red tip bush only to discover a large cucumber curved in form like a club.

"Andrea, look at this!"

We had been wondering whether or not a second cucumber was playing hide and seek amidst our lush full garden where we had found the first just a few days ago. Last night Andrea used our homegrown cucumbers and cherry tomatoes in a salad. We beamed like two proud parents. I never realized the joy we could garnish from a small garden plot.

She then harvested a brilliant bouquet of fragrant roses and large yellow mums to brighten her workplace with these treasures.

"I brought fresh flowers every week to work and often gave some to colleagues to brighten their day," she reported. "I know they'll love these flowers!"

My heart filled with satisfaction at the thought of her learning to appreciate the simple wonders of making everyday life a place of beauty and rest with flowers from our gardens. My weekend garden is becoming our daily delight. This one wee plot of cultivated land has now extended beyond its meager borders to five other areas in the front and back yards. In fact, Andrea designed one featured area in the front of our house by herself. When you drive past our home, you can see the colors she chose splashed among the red bark: vibrant yellow mum-like daisies, brilliant orange lilies, and red geraniums intermingled with red ground cover.

Another garden area I cultivate is a collection of pots decorating our patio. Many rest in rustic, wooden wagons and flower carts. Others perch proudly on plant stands. I enjoyed tilling the earth in order to create a rich blend of mulch from raw earth and potting soil. I plant the brilliant flowers in arrangements in the same way a painter designs on canvas.

The warm weather lured me to begin preparations for this outside retreat. My husband hung a decorative wall fountain, recently purchased. A small pitcher at the top pours water into a series of clay bowls as it circulates. The sound of running water joined a chorus of birds chirping from treetops. Spring is in the air and I envision hours spent writing from the patio swing.

I love to garden, designing the earth into delightful nooks. There is a patch of land in the very back of our yard off to one side and almost hidden from view. This is my rose garden—a private escape—where I sit on the bench nestled under a large maple tree admiring the surrounding flowers. The majestic maple has grown so large that it now covers the rose garden rendering it useless for producing. I saw the inevitable moving of my rose bushes when last year's yield was quite pathetic. However, finding a new spot proves difficult with grass and flowerbeds covering most of the land.

I eyed a section in my rose garden sizing up how many pots I could fit into the forefront. This is a sunny spot conducive for growing vegetables. "Adding pots will prove delightful to the eye," I write from the swing. Today I will kill the crab grass encroaching upon the land and then prepare for moving pots. Growing vegetables renews my sense of childhood having worked in our family garden with my mother. This love of gardening definitely stems from her childhood influence.

I love to grow vegetables because in doing so I experience the cyclic nature of life. Each day I explore the plants for new surprises hiding behind leaves. I feel a closeness to the earth and to my Creator when I garden. There is a time for preparing the soil, a time for planting, and a time for reaping. As the summer moves aside and the crispness of fall ushers in, my garden slumbers. The frigid winter soon forces one to rest from all labor.

The joy of gardening will forever be a part of my life even if merely a few herb plants populate the sunny area behind kitchen sink. As I age and the weariness of body prohibits the tilling of earth, I will still delight in snipping off brittle sprigs from houseplants. To garden is to celebrate life, to create with vigor, and to commune with peace.

God's serenity resonates from flowers even though they are silent. The creative soul drinks in this peacefulness along with eye-catching colors. Gardening inspires this eclectic creative with ideas for poems, prose, artwork, and songs. This humble art form reminds my human soul of the inevitable cycle of life as I prepare to return to the earth from which I came. With this understanding, my artistic soul lives each day more appreciative knowing I must create before meeting the Creator.

THE WONDER OF CREATIVITY

I awoke in the middle of the night with the following dialogue going through my mind: "He waited at a distance so as to not disturb the couple's repose—even if it wasn't him, with her." It seemed to be part of a novel or movie script. I wrote it down and will save it even though I'm not yet a novel writer. Random in nature, this occurrence does not surprise me. In fact, nothing as far as creative emergences does these days. Since writing every morning for almost four years, I have witnessed so many unique ways in which inspiration comes to my artistic soul bringing immeasurable delight as I learn to laugh at my human condition.

During a recent conversation with my daughter, an avid artist and writer, she explained the unexpected onslaughts of novel dialogue, which flood her mind right before falling asleep. I listened in amazement never thinking for one moment that this would ever be my experience. The desire to write novels has not appealed to me in the least. Then a few weeks later, I awake with this dialogue running through my thoughts. Perhaps creativity in one begets similar ideas in another.

My other daughter, an avid artist and dance choreographer, explained her creative emergences with, "I cannot help myself! When the ideas and desires begin to flow, I just have to pursue the art form as soon as possible." She has a hankering to cartoon again. Before this conversation, I had shared a new addition to the musical for youth coming to me in pieces. Even as I spoke, she began seeing the choreography in her mind. After school, I witnessed her creative mental magic at work once again during the ballroom dance class we teach for seventh and eighth grade youth. Like a painter with human forms, she stopped to capture the artistic movements in her mind and then explain them to the rest of us waiting in silence.

I am quite fortunate to have many women in my family who are creative eclectics. They dabble in diverse art forms as free spirits and love life more because of possessing and practicing these traits. Weekly, their spontaneous and delightful lives amaze as they produce a surplus of artistic wonders from which others find encouragement and amusement. I often write down their witty comments and unceasing dialogue as I try to capture the cleverness of the moment. Together we provide an informal support group for nurturing our imaginations and practicing our various art forms.

Living life as a creative soul proves to delight daily. The beholder's eyes open to a muse others often unknowingly pass right over. For instance, my daughter and I turned a trip to the market into a mini stroll through a floral shop by lingering to admire the array of floral and plant displays. We must have spent twenty minutes admiring the multi-color tulips in buttery yellow, snowy white, and flaming orange hues. Fuchsia pink and periwinkle blue hydrangeas filled our eyes. Nature's expressions adorned human creations as flowers poised in baskets and vases of various forms. I could not take my gaze off an arrangement of bubble gum pink miniature roses mixed with tiny white carnation-like flowers. Interspersed English ivy spilled over the sides of Paris-like vases mentally transporting me to a French café. As we perused, I took mental notes for new container gardening ideas.

Creativity also helps us to laugh at our human condition. For example, yesterday's writing produced a personal experience essay highlighting the humorous side of weight struggles for middle-aged women. I chuckled over the ideas pouring forth as they made their way into computer text like mischievous children returning with spoils from the neighbor's garden. Utilizing real-life, frustrating events for writing fuel turned episodes of depression into an amusing retreat. Whether this piece ever incites the chuckle of another didn't matter in that moment. Merely to have fun provided ample motivation. Of course, my mother's positive response to this piece greatly satisfied as well:

> I did enjoy the piece (and there were no calories). I saw a program on TV that said when you are born a chubby baby, the fat cells never leave but go into hiding with tremendous patience while they wait for you to get middle aged! Then we are challenged beyond our wildest imagination, what a fight; my 11lb birth weight has taken its toll on this elderly woman. A man of tremendous willpower, my husband has met his Waterloo. He was the cutest chubby baby ever, and now he is sporting a muffin-top. Every dog has his or her day. I love you. Mom

This morning I marvel over how different my mindset is since those early days as a serious missionary and pastor's wife. Rarely did I laugh at random volleys of wit. Now it does not take much to entertain me. A cleverly crafted romantic comedy provides amusement as the rigors of living reduce to something one can laugh about rather than staying up all night worrying about. Life used to be intensely serious and I viewed God in much the same way. I now muse over how I must have appeared to my Creator whose candor is reflected in scripture, "Laughter is good medicine." He obviously finds humor in the human plight or why would He engineer menopause for aging women? This is a time when inexplicable desires to make a last go at influencing one's world mix with irritability that paralyzes all positive attempts; it is also a season of life when night sweats tempt even the most prudent to run down the street naked.

He must have had a sense of humor when He reversed the passions of men and woman; the young male and forty-year-old woman ablaze with desire, while the young mother and aging man prefer periods of abstinence; the mother to nurture her children and the father to watch football games. For the creative spirit, so many of life's mysteries and perplexities are harvestable for writing to bring humor and meaning to living.

Yesterday my daughter shared a friend's inquiry into our family's faith and compatibility. I could not help but wonder whether one day women such as her roommate will read my musings in book form. Could the tapestry of my life include youthful readers who have barely embarked upon their journey through stage II? This is the time promptly following sorority life when the rigors of marriage and family leave young adults wondering why they ever signed up for this life class. I would not put it past God to weave this irony into the latter part of my life. In fact, it would greatly please me to hear of women any age learning to laugh, believe, and create because of something I wrote. Maybe some of them will also pick up their pens and open their art sets a little earlier in life as they explore the wonders of creativity.

Practicing Creative Prudence

As I reflect and write, the awareness of another learning principle comes to mind. Be cautious how much you share with others concerning your bountiful array of productivity. Few can tolerate hearing about it unless the person is also a creative eclectic. Your sharing will come across as boastful and overwhelming. I have learned this the hard way with others withdrawing from me after I flooded their minds with too many details. Remember that others have full lives and do not need to know what flips your idea switch. Only those curious enough to pursue you with questions should receive answers; even then, mete out meager portions in order to avoid overload. Your mind may never stop conjuring up ideas, but others do not share your disposition and to them you have become an overwhelming force they would rather avoid than engage. Only give your creativity away to those trustworthy and of a kindred spirit.

I know all too well how lonely this life can be when you contain all of your excitement inside. My husband refers to himself as a "lone wolf" who has learned self-contentment. His example inspires me to find peace as a lone wolf as well. In fact, I have learned that living in this lonely place provides a lot of time and mental energy for pouring into my dreams. Instead of pitying myself for the lack of friends yearning to hear of my latest venture, I pour my creativity onto pages and into art forms. Perhaps one of the most foundational reasons I decided to write this book was to let others know they are not alone. My intent is to share with those sharing the make-up of this kind of artistic personality. People who may have felt odd and alone all of their lives can finally receive the reassurance that there are others out there with much the same wiring as them.

Although I am used to doing most projects by myself, I have learned to draw inspiration from other artistic people around me. I often realign with right perspectives when thinking about my mother who continues to create well into her seventies. Her example of enjoying so many different expressions without ambitions to become wealthy or popular keep me grounded in terms of what is most important in life. She is a giver who continually looks for recipients for her overflow of projects. I remember my father's love of working with wood that has inspired the building of two houses and multiple birdhouses. Even now, at the age of seventy-seven, he is overseeing the conversion of another garage into a family room. He delights in always having a project to do. When I am feeling lonely from my solo flight, I also remember my sister, Gina. Her excitement when sharing her latest sketch reminds me that the joy is in the act of making something new.

Perhaps this book will help those who lack others with which to share their passions. If you find your way into these pages alone, I applaud your brave soul seeking to explore innate gifting solo. I hope you find the confidence, creativity, and courage you seek. To you, I write these pages in hopes you will draw strength from my experiences and others highlighted in this book. For the creative eclectic must live free from burdensome demands in order to allow personal expression to emerge. As you seek your own unique path, separate the "jobs to make money" from the "freedom to live." Begin today endeavoring to pursue your creative urges merely because it is delightful and in some mysterious ways makes you feel alive!

THE CREATIVE STAGE

Some would say I am all over the map and not focused enough on one pursuit. However, I am in the creative stage of my destiny and creative stages need to be broad in order to allow for exploration, change, and flux. Turning of direction or refinement of purpose will come in time. I will not rush this present stage of discovery. What a blessed time when the entire world of giftedness is my oyster. As I experiment with different writing and art forms, consulting pursuits and business ventures, I sense my capacity expanding to unbelievable parameters. Yet, I daily return to a place of reflection. Here, God speaks mysteries to my spirit and my hand records them with pen into the leather journal given to me as a gift from a student.

Why do I love writing more than any other pursuit in life? My writing is unique to me and therefore, no one can claim it. It is my personal expression free from the control of others. When I write, I know no bounds! Writing helps me to define who I am and what I want, and it helps me form possible paths for pursuing the emerging ambitions. Writing helps me to navigate this creative stage in order to taste those tantalizing ideas mentally even before they appear in human form, after which I can assist their delivery by writing them into forms of possible practice. Conversely, writing helps me to discover which activities do not mesh with my personal desires so I can eliminate them.

This creative stage is delightful in terms of exploration. Like a piñata spilling forth with candy, I gleefully sort through the possibilities wide-eyed. I could not do this without the tool of daily writing. I have found this practice important for sustaining life pursuits whether recovering from codependency, building careers, or developing a practice of writing. Allowing many options to present before sifting and deciding which to keep is possible during this creative stage.

In the long run, I am glad that I have invited this stage of sampling creativity in various forms. Some artistic expressions have nicely integrated into my life while I tossed others aside. The emergence of writing and digital designing as this season's main fanfare fills my days with happiness and satisfaction. I do not know what the future holds in terms of adding new artistic expressions but when another creative stage descends, I will enjoy the opportunity to explore once again.

EXERCISE

Try something new this week. Select an art form or activity you've never done but feel inexplicably drawn to doing. If you hit a creative block, take a stroll through an arts and craft store to stir your artistic juices.

CHAPTER 6

REFRESHING CREATIVITY

THROUGH EXCURSIONS

*"The human spirit needs places where nature has
not been rearranged by human hands."*

—*anonymous*

CREATIVE EXCURSIONS

Travel excursions provide healthy ways to revitalize creative
energy, which is vital to keeping a flow of innovation. Try
connecting visits to a new place with opportunities to appreciate
nature. Sometimes, you must go out in search of inspiration when a
muse calls to your heart. My husband and I promised each other we
would schedule regular times for exploration because travel excursions allow us to stir our creativity again when our careers flatline
our insights and energy.

We just returned from one such getaway to the Grand Canyon.
We stayed in the quaint town of Williams, Arizona and rode the
Grand Railroad train up to the Canyon and back. We feasted our
eyes on the staggering beauty of this national wonder, taking
pictures that pale in comparison to what the naked eye witnessed.

A hushed silence resonates through soul, mind, and spirit when you peer into this vast crevasse. All worries melt away when standing on the edge of this precipice. The end-of-day pictures turned out the best, with sunrays illuminating the canyon's rows of browns, oranges, and amber hues. Eagles soared through the expansive gap as onlookers snapped pictures and sighed.

Back in Williams, we enjoyed a hearty barbeque, live music, and engaging conversation with local merchants and international travelers. The aroma of smoke wafted through outdoor restaurants in a Wild West atmosphere, transporting diners back to simpler times. We wandered the streets, taking pictures of Old West reenactments. There was the mini gold mining town, with a selection of buildings created in the theme of that era, such as a jail with the bars, wood cot, and gun props. This short excursion is one of many for us. We have been contemplating the brevity of life and the amount of energy we spend working, and we decided to make some important changes.

When our occupations encroach on our mental sanity, our hearts long for nature's majesty. We give so much to our careers that we find a mild depression regularly descending if we don't treat ourselves enough. Both of our parents raised us to appreciate the great outdoors and a lure towards adventure. Recently, a desire to rediscover our childhood delights became too strong to ignore any longer. After returning from our Grand Canyon trip, we rested before reengaging in the work force. Today a sense of peace permeates our otherwise taxed minds. In addition, the fresh perspective we gained from the excursion allows us to align priorities, as the holidays loom on the horizon this brisk autumn day in late September. We will create a magical world of wonder in our home for family and friends to enjoy this Thanksgiving and Christmas with pictures from our recent travels to the Grand Canyon.

Our time on earth speeds by, regardless of whether we pursue our dreams or not. Children grow up quickly and, before we know it, we sit pining for their brief visits or the occasional times we can visit with family and friends. Even as older age rapidly approaches, we can rediscover the child within who never ages.

While writing this piece, I rediscovered an anniversary card I gave to my husband. The photograph is of a little boy and girl holding hands while walking to the end of a lake pier, fishing poles in arms and bait baskets, almost dragging the ground, slung over shoulders. Their tiny jeans are accented by the boy's cherry-red flannel shirt and Christmas-green ball cap. Tiny fishing floats bob from their fishing poles above them in the wind. My heart swelled with appreciation over this poignant visual message, communicating what I try to describe here with words. Within each one of us is a child full of wonder and eagerness to explore our glorious world. Yes, this sense of discovery imparted in childhood draws my husband and I to return to the things that give us life.

Family trips come to mind. Jobs that didn't pay much but offered rich enjoyment. As we enter our fifties, we realize that life must be lived with ample time given to family, friends, and excursions into nature. Priorities must be adjusted in order to finance getaways, homespun holidays, and luxurious walks through gardens. We must find what brings us life and ink these activities into crowded calendar pages.

We look to the Lifegiver of all Lifegivers through spiritual excursions in the form of prayer, meditation, and an active looking for God in all—since He is, after all, the ultimate Life source.

TREASURE HUNTING

Developing creativity begins with the realization that life is too short not to make time for you! It continues with courting your inner artist with inspirationally fun activities. My sister calls it treasure hunting. I find the practice enchanting. We peruse discount stores for reduce-priced "finds" that call to our artists' souls. Often, themes develop as we delight in the visual array. As we add items to the basket, we discuss possible ways to use them. No censoring of ideas is allowed at this point. Later, we sift and sort, leaving nearly all the pieces behind. It would not be a treasure hunt unless only select items made it through our screening process. More importantly, we enjoy each other while developing an "eye for design."

My sister and I began treasure hunting long ago when we had our arts and craft business. We searched for unique artifacts in discount stores to embellish our country and Victorian home décor line. We added them to the "one-of-a-kind" creations saved for the bi-annual home boutiques, while items we produced in multiples were to be distributed to southern California stores. The one-of-a kind creations were the most fun, while reproducing multiples meant no varying in design, thus robbing us of our creative joy. This lesson imprinted an important reality into our hearts and minds that we still draw from as artists, writers, and educators. We must continue creating innovatively.

The child-like place inside of us longs for spontaneity. To cultivate a life of creativity, our treasure hunts must freely include time to play through designing. Sometimes a boyish quality emerges inside of me, originating from working outside with my father. While mom and sis were sewing and cooking, I preferred helping dad. Two sprinkler systems and a stone path later, the love of "hands on" activities continues to flourish.

Treasure hunting can also include finding interesting people. Recently, my husband and I visited Venus Beach where we enjoyed taking pictures of unique individuals. One of my favorites was a man dressed up like a tree with an old fishing net that had seashells attached. My husband loves portrait photography, while I prefer scenery and up-close nature pictures. When we uploaded our treasures onto our computers, his were primarily of people while mine were of sea, birds, and sailboats.

We also revisited the Yosemite Valley where we went on our honeymoon. The raw nature calls to my heart. We tasted this recently with a day trip to the Kern River. Our digital cameras snapped the raging rapids, odd shaped trees, and river rafters in-route. Treasure-hunting outings into nature are especially enjoyable, but even a quick excursion to my backyard garden also delights.

Treasure hunting provides the spice to life. It gives the artistic soul just the shot of energy needed in order to make it through the mundane and difficult "have to's." You can enjoy treasure hunting with others or venture out alone. The value is not in multiple and costly purchases but in attuning your senses to what brings you delight.

WHEN CREATIVITY CALLS

Last Sunday, I went to the local Poppy Festival in order to go where creative people gather—something I have found feeds my artistic side. I just needed to find new inspiration. The sights and sounds filled my senses as I joined the other attendees funneling through the open gate. I do not know why this compulsion to visit a festival I had often skipped in the past increased with intensity as the weekend drew near, but rationalizing away the idea just did not work any longer, so I acquiesced to the little girl in me, tugging on my hand and giving me an inkling of treasure awaiting.

Someone thrust a festival map into my hand while sunlight nearly blinded my view. Upon opening the guide, my eyes quickly tracked along the pathways until finding the Arts and Crafts sections. *Aha* ricocheted through my mind as an unseen force propelled me forward. I made my way through what I deemed peripheral pleasures, such as the food court, aerospace exhibit (no scientist here), and commercial booths. Neither the sumptuous barbeque aromas nor the squeals of delighted children tempted today. I was a woman on a mission!

Then I saw the field of artistic delights in all her glory, spread across an expansive section with patchwork quilts of canvas coverings. Wind chimes crackled in breezes; swirling hair ribbons in magical motion tempted fresh-faced little girls aspiring to be princesses for the day. I moved quickly through the crowded, grassy isles knowing the time for indulging my senses was limited. Guests would gather at my home for a birthday BBQ within two hours. With a small purse firmly clasped under arm, I wove my way through the crowds, only stopping at the booths that called to me.

The first was an enchanted land created by two polymer clay artists, a mother and daughter team. Intricately adorned vases displayed delicate meandering clay vines accented with miniature flowers. Magical masks stared with vacant eyes. Ribbons sailed in the wind. I stopped to read the quotes on refrigerator magnets selecting two for future inspiration: "Imagination is more important than knowledge," by Albert Einstein and "To accomplish great things, we must not only act but also dream," by Anatole France.

The idea of carving my own quotes into clay one day tempted me. Rich hues of purple, lavender, rose, and red astounded me, and I was delighted by intricate designs so tiny one could barely focus on their form, let alone carve them into clay. We spoke of sculpture and I asked about how their talents emerged. I do not know what fascinated me more: the art pieces they produced or the creative relationship they enjoyed. This artistic mother, transferring her talent and passion to her offspring, reminded me of my own heritage. In the midst of bubbling discussion, a granddaughter emerged. I watched as the young mother took out a finely crafted doll she had purchased at the fair. The little girl lit up as she gently stroked the yarn hair.

"Is this your daughter?" I inquired.

"Yes," her mother returned.

"She sits right by us and sculptures," the grandmother crooned.

My fascination with their creative lineage increased as they shared how the little girl also works with clay. My heart warmed with the fire of three generations sharing a passion for an art form I know all too well to be tedious and exacting. Father Time chimed inside my head as I quickly paid for my purchases and swept off to the next intrigue.

A wildcat's greenish-yellow eyes locked my gaze from across the aisle. Piercing eyes met viewers, providing a feel for the hunt as if these creatures stalked you. This booth belonged to an artist who painted wild animals and domestic pets. She enraptured audiences with tales of photography seasons in open animal parks among wild beasts with only a trainer between. I marveled as much over her photography, displayed on cards in a cylinder rack, as the wild paintings hanging. She eagerly answered my questions concerning technique with vivid descriptions of the steps taken to create such masterpieces. Her generous spirit was interrupted when a voice called to me:

"Mrs. Luna?"

One of my former students, walking with her parents, had spotted me. We shared excitedly as the artist sold her wares to other customers. The mother noticed a painting that resembled their beloved boxer, and I watched in astonishment as the two animal lovers disappeared into an enchanted land of dogs. Their passion for pets closely resembled the passion I feel for my artwork and writing. This experience made me realize how creative raising pets can be. The offer to do animal portraits was met with eager questions as the parent poured through the artist's portfolio pages.

One glance at my watch reminded me that the passage of time waits for no artistic interaction. From across the field, I spied the work of an artist I had visited at another local street fair. Frank Dixon is a watercolorist who works as a high school and college art teacher. He creates enchanting, tree-like creatures hiding in mystical forests. He explained how his own emotions often reflect back from their grins and groans. I shared how the cards I had purchased from him enamored my students. He pointed out his new book filled with art lessons for youth and an accompanying CD with video lessons.

I knew most assuredly that I was a loyal customer once again. We spoke of technique, publishing, website designing, and art lessons. I shared about this book, which highlights the creative eclectic. His interest peaked because of a similar project he had created. Our exchange of ideas propelled each of us further in our quest for creativity. His artwork and self-publishing pursuits intrigued me, while he was interested in my knowledge of web design software and possible marketing applications. We mutually benefited from fresh insights to advance our artistic goals.

The two hours passed quickly as I wove through the crowd to find the festival entrance once again. The time had been grand indeed, and I had a purse full of pleasures to take home as reminders. In addition to the memories and new resources gleaned, I noted the need to make festivals a permanent part of my artistic exploration. Perhaps these special people will never cross my path of life again, but just for today, they provided essential scaffolding for my own artistic climb. I hope the exchange was mutual.

Through this day's experiences, I have learned to obey the longing to explore, regardless of whether my mind argues to the contrary. Obeying these urges and daring to move past the mundane demands of life is profitable for the creative eclectic. Whenever I defy the nonessentials and follow my creative impulse, I discover delightful experiences, people, and art. Most importantly, I celebrate the exchange of creativity from artist to artist that comes from following the muse when she calls.

EPIPHANY

Sometimes creative encouragement appears when you least expect it. A chance encounter with a kindred artistic spirit happens, and you feel your heart redirected towards what is most important. Often I meet complete strangers while my husband and I are on our creative excursions. These conversations refresh my creativity and hone my direction. The following is an account of such an experience.

> Epiphany 1. Sudden realization
> A sudden intuitive leap of understanding, especially through an ordinary but striking occurrence
> - It came to him in an epiphany what his life's work was to be (Encarta Dictionary: English - North America).

The word "epiphany" flowed from her mouth, describing the "knowing" present when a work of art comes forth. We were two artistic souls who met randomly and shared a serendipitous encounter that would change the course of my life forever. The morning after experiencing this unexpected camaraderie, I now lie in bed, gazing out of the window at the rippling Colorado River. I write from the eighth floor of the Tropicana Hotel in Laughlin, Nevada. My husband and children left yesterday while I stayed in order to drive to Vegas today and meet up with my niece's bachelorette party. Staying alone was unsettling until the older woman with the sparkling eyes stopped to chat.

I was walking around looking for a coffee kiosk when I ran into her again. We had met the night before while my daughter and I danced. Her son was the drummer for the band. She is a stylish, sixty-five year old art teacher. We got talking about teaching and hobbies, and I shared that I was an aspiring writer working on several manuscripts. I learned that she is a painter who used to work in the graphics design world for a television company. She explained how the long hours took their toll and that, at the age of fifty, she decided to change careers and use her Bachelors of Fine Art to teach. She revealed that it took twelve years, while raising children, to complete her degree. The only position available was 5th grade, so she has been in the same school for the last fifteen years. She will retire in a year or two.

She is so full of life that her face radiates. We spoke of the artist's temperament, and she laughingly called it "borderline bi-polar." We laughed over our tendencies to go into manic moods of exhilaration as a new project sucks us into its vortex. We mused over the ensuing depression as we plummet into self-pity and self-loathing. The driven, obsessive behavior that craves perfection and creates madness that never allows us to settle on a project's finality as you go back to tweak "just one last area."

How wonderful it was to hear the words of wisdom pouring forth from an artist in her golden years. She spoke of the "grind" side of painting. These are the times when one must push through even though the craft grows difficult. She commented on the plight of women from her generation and mine as society relegates our art to exploration as hobbyists. "For in this mindset," she explained, "creating can only be pursued after the sheets are changed, dishes done, and children tucked into bed." Sadly, a woman's "me time" often fills with duties making it impossible to perform artistically while waiting on families. In contrast, we marveled over the younger artists who give themselves permission to pursue their craft.

I, in turn, shared the steps I have taken to carve out creative time; rising early for writing, spending weekends and holidays enmeshed in projects. She seemed to admire my progress in pursuing my passions. I shared what it took to establish patterns that other family members respected, such as uninterrupted morning writing. We sighed over the demands of teaching that leave us wrung out and void of emotional and mental strength at day's end.

I shared my dream of publishing. Speaking the words to a stranger seemed to cement them in my heart and mind. I told her about my websites for marketing my books and how I have taken online lessons to learn web design. Surprise struck me when she gingerly asked, "Would it be too forward to get your email address so we can keep in touch?" The possibility of her one day reading my books seemed an honor of the highest magnitude.

Wow! A complete stranger sent along my path to reassure my direction. She even wrapped her mind around possible organizational structures for my books. I told her of my confusion as to separating poetry from prose, essays, and narrative. As an avid reader, she reassured me that books contain all kinds of combinations with poetry. She also suggested that the same poetry could be in more than one book that I write. I told her that publishing would be worth the money and effort if only for my posterity and the students who I try to inspire to write.

This woman with knowing eyes is the third such encounter in recent weeks from other artists who want to link. My heart is warm with hope this morning as I write. A quiet knowing radiates from the smile I imagine on God's face. Another step along the path of destiny unfolded and one more encounter closer to my quest of becoming a published writer.

PHOTOGRAPHY EXCURSIONS

In these financially tight times, photography excursions are a poor man's vacation! Hobbies take the edge off life and venturing out to new places fills the creative eclectic's photo bank, which enhances the imagination! As a career educator, I need a lot of "me time" after "work time." Teaching challenging students is often like standing before a tough crowd at a comedy café. You use your best lines, but the youthful equivalency of rotten tomatoes splatter all over your face: rolled eyes, blurted wisecracks, and mocking gestures. I try not to wince or let them know when they get to me. Students have a crowd too, in the form of the other kids who sit around laughing at their antics. By week's end, I really need a break.

One of my favorite hobbies is exploring places that inspire my creativity. There are relatively inexpensive trips you can enjoy that will provide photos to serve as blog posts, ideas for artwork, or inspiration for writing. While my husband and I sometimes plan these mini vacations months in advance, at times they are spur of the moment.

For example, one Valentine's Day Sunday, we decided on a creative gift for each other that was low-cost and thoroughly enjoyable. We visited the Getty Museum in Malibu, California. The tickets were free if you booked ahead online. Both of us felt that familiar tug of a photography excursion, and this seemed like just the right outing for us.

We had already visited the Getty in Los Angeles and had found the experience very refreshing. Fountains percolated up and rained down, soothing our minds and souls. We enjoyed the outside gardens. As a flower lover, I honed in on unique flowers and foliage that caught my eye. Unusual trees sparked my interest, and I found myself studying their unique twisted shapes. Sculptured bushes and trellises were true works of art.

The Malibu Getty did not disappoint. This Getty features various museums with art from different eras such as the Roman and Greek periods. Visitors can take photos of most exhibits but the museum forbids the use of tripods or flash photography. I was particularly interested in eyes that day, studying how a painter captured light and emotion in them. My husband, on the other hand, was transfixed with the body sculptures.

Other photography excursions have included towns and cities throughout California such as the picturesque Napa Valley, San Francisco, Carmel, and Lake Tahoe. Wherever we go, we take pictures, which fuel my creativity for months afterwards. I enjoy editing them using Photoshop, giving them as framed gifts, or using them in blog posts.

These outings also provide a fresh perspective. Once we leave our careers behind, the problems we obsess over seem to disappear and become insignificant. Our life together and love of photography and travel becomes paramount. New dreams for the future ignite in our hearts, and we permanently alter our choices to those more beneficial for our welfare. Returning home isn't difficult because we remember there is a grander world out there than any worries we may have back home.

EXERCISE

Plan a creative excursion. Decide to venture outside of your usual comfort zone and visit a new place.

CHAPTER 7

PURSUING LIFESTYLE CREATIVITY

"Imagination is more important than knowledge."
-Albert Einstein

VALUE ANALYSIS

Pursuing lifestyle creativity is about finding out what you are good at and finding resources to support you in developing your gifts. This is about more than simply discovering whether you are an artist, writer or musician; pursuing lifestyle creativity entails finding the balance between artistic pursuits and career obligations. Achieving and maintaining this balance is precarious at best, for you must be two things equally. You must also be practical about life's demands, like paying the bills, and intertwine your "real life" with your "artistic life."

To determine your destiny as a creative person, an intense analysis of values is in order. For me, the highest felt need on my list is freedom to spend my "outside-of-career" time the way I want. I discovered this value during my years in recovery as the enabler of an addict. Part of the Twelve Steps is to write a personal inventory in order to focus on your own issues and not on those of the addict. To my surprise, I realized I directed most of my energy towards helping others versus developing what I loved. I spent years writing in order to find out what I truly valued and desired. It was during these years that the pull towards becoming a writer began to stir deep within me.

This process of value determination continued as I began to explore my history and life patterns further. You see, I have lived most of my life in survival. No "freebies" existed as I was growing up. I was expected to earn any spending money desired. My years as a missionary and pastor's wife years were lean, both overseas and stateside. After a messy divorce, I entered the life of single parenting and building a new career.

Therefore, I cannot think of a time during my entire life when I experienced financial freedom. I never enjoyed lavishly creating, free from worries about responsibilities; earning a living sucked most of the creative life out of me. With this history in mind, is it any wonder that freedom is high on my value list? I am just too old to come under the control of another person or system again. I would gladly forgo fame and fortune in lieu of the freedom to create as I wish.

I also enjoy seeing other people light up with artistic passions. I aspire to put a spark to the wicks of innovation that are often smoldered due to life's responsibilities. I love to see faces radiate with wonder as people design and create, whether they are using tangible mediums or digital tools. I have repeatedly witnessed the human spirit's delight in releasing the imagination. What creative eclectic does not love bringing a brainchild into the world?

Since I value freedom and the joy of igniting creativity in others, I resolve to choose paths that will enable me to share what I have learned about creativity with others. Instead of becoming the mighty published writer that others swoon over and admire, I long to show other aspiring writers that it is possible for anyone to publish by taking the self-publishing path. Anyone can present their voice to the world by designing their own website as well.

During the quest to discover my personal values, I have gleaned a few gold nuggets of wisdom, but to be honest, the process is rather tedious and time-consuming. Perhaps the most essential life change I made was to implement those times of regular reflection that I discussed previously. After a few years at this practice, I now consistently see pieces of my destiny puzzle emerging in the strangest ways and at the most unexpected times. If my philosophy is that everyone can create and express their talents in the world, then I try to choose a path that will provide easy-to-follow steps along the way, and journaling is something that anyone can do.

Sometimes a value emerges while doing something I discover I do not like. This provides contrast—and I often discover what I love by identifying what I do not. For instance, I get frustrated with the time it takes to learn how to paint, so I use Photoshop to digitally alter photos. In the classroom, I get as bored as my students do with paper and pencil activities, so I create user-friendly, flash animated learning games. These experiences help me to see that one of my main values is innovation.

I have also discovered my values by noticing those activities that bring satisfaction. I enjoy working in team-planning situations in which other creative and practical people pool their ideas and expertise. Planning teams enable me to function in my areas of creative strength due to freedom from worrying about specific implementation steps. In fact, my personal (versus career) projects often languish without forward momentum because I wrestle with them alone. If not for my husband and best friend's consistent listening and reflecting back to me what they hear me saying, I would move forward at a much slower pace. Recently, a colleague and I have decided to work on some joint writing projects. We meet regularly to share our progress on co-authored work and then we discuss our own projects. This collaboration and encouragement propels our writing forward.

When selecting the people you will trust with your creative projects, it is essential that they are encouragers by nature. A critical person or an insecure person who is threatened by your successes will eventually shut down your confidence and creativity. Look for people who value processing ideas together. I make sure they are respectful, self-assured, and trustworthy. I do not like people trying to take control of my ideas or projects. Rather, I look for people who help me to develop them and focus on the possible process steps.

Whether or not you find support for your creativity, you can develop what you love to do if you are persistent at reserving time for yourself. Determine your creative values and then vehemently guard them. In time, opportunities will arise that suit your particular art forms.

ENGAGING REAL LIFE

The emerging writer or artist cannot always find career paths which aptly suit his or her talents. However, there are still ample reasons to pursue creativity. The very nature of these gifts is to translate human feelings and thoughts into a new perspective. Lessons gleaned from life's bleak valleys transform into songs of promise sung from mountaintops. To look for inspiration merely along rose-strewn paths is an exaggeration of life's finest and fairest at the expense of most people's reality, for if the writer or artist never experiences the bleak paths of human existence, how can he or she voice those experiences for others?

Creative souls, like everyone, must walk paths of the mundane and languish in emotions in order to capture the essence of the human struggle. When this turmoil translates into art forms that become a beacon of hope, we become change agents in our world! What better place to marry the divine with the human than in a career? Working to pay the bills alongside others who are, likewise, working to pay the bills, tends to strip away posturing. We become quite aware of our humanness. From this place of honesty, we write and create that which encourages and inspires.

As an avid Christian reader, I'm wary of devotionals void of personal experience examples. Having over thirty years of faith under my belt makes me quite familiar with the scripture; however, when I read an author's gut wrenching sharing, I find it possible to weep as easily as to soar. I want to know how they applied their faith out in the real world. This kind of honesty touches me deeply.

So today, I choose to take the path less traveled that marries real life with creativity—the one that doesn't clamor after fame and fortune. I choose to seek my Lord's gentle guidance while following behind His steps as illuminated by His Spirit. Today I seek to live life in the fullest way I presently know how to do. When creative ideas splash upon the canvas of my real world experiences, I will take up the tools for developing whatever they present in that moment, whether that tool is a pen for writing, a camera for capturing images, a computer for designing, or art supplies for creating. With the eagerness of a child, I will explore, first for me and then as an example for others, what it means to navigate creativity's path while balancing work and real life.

CREATIVE MAINTENANCE

How do I keep creativity alive and flourishing in the midst of life's practical demands? This question came to mind this morning and begged answering. Foremost to me is the early morning writing as the practice seems to clear the cobwebs that find their way into my mind and soul. Where there are webs, there are spiders in the form of spinning thoughts, unrestrained insecurities, unbridled fears, and distorted perspectives. Writing each morning helps to purge these emotional tormentors. Then, my spirit and emotions seem open to devotional interaction with the Creator, the author and finisher of my faith.

Insights frequently visit me throughout the day through an inspired thought, a timely word, an artistic object, or a unique situation. Having connected to my Creator in the morning, I am sensitive to these unexpected delights during the day. Like Dorothy visiting the Wizard of Oz, my curiosity seduces me to look behind the curtain of situations to see the root cause.

However, what are we to do with the myriad of practical demands that tug on us: the doctor's appointment, car servicing, banking, shopping, etc.? These demands are a contrasting bore, but the maintenance of both practical life and creative development require responsible actions.

I find it helpful to pace the scheduling of "have to tasks." For instance, one week may be for the doctor's appointment then the next for the car servicing. If I plan too many tasks all in one week, I find my spirit dampened by the time demands that leave little time to create. I also take my current writing notebook and inspirational book along. The amount of time our "to do" lists require is staggering. I prefer to accomplish the mundane and explore the creative all in the same sitting.

Creative maintenance also applies to relationships. Because I am a teacher, I do have time off during the summer or winter breaks. However, my tendency is to over schedule these times with family and friends in an attempt to play catch up. I have learned to stagger time with people and creative projects. My greatest challenge comes from believing my artistic projects are worth pursuing. Once this understanding became an intrinsic part of who I am, then calling my family and friends back after writing time seems normal to all.

Dichotomy

The artist creates for the sake of creating
The educator creates for youth

The artist craves personal expression
The educator often concedes expression for impact

The artist knows no bounds of imagining
The educator functions within constraints

The artist needs living
The educator gives life

The world cries for both
While both cry within

This dichotomy is the foundational concept on which I built my websites. I have struggled with these two sides of myself, which sometimes neatly coexist while at other times go to war with one another. The creative spirit feels much like a willful child who compulsively runs into the rain and stomps in puddles, while the educator stands at the threshold yelling, "Come back and put on your raincoat and boots!"

The artist does not often tolerate "no" and if she does, much sulking and tantrums result. The educator's understanding of functioning within constraints makes her an indomitable spirit. The artist easily bruises and slinks into shadows of disapproval while the educator stands firmly to fight wars of injustice.

This morning I wonder, "How many other artist/educators function with this inner conflict?" When I think about the time and effort needed to create and maintain websites, integrating the artist and educator online seems like an overwhelming proposition. But then again, the artist can play while the educator forms structure and reliability. The artist fuels the innovation while the educator organizes and edits. Perhaps God knew what He was doing when He created this dichotomy in me. I sent this piece to my best friend, Barbie, and found her reaction encouraging:

> How interesting this piece is to me as I re-read it. You just described "us." This dichotomy is the essence of "us"...you are living in the world as an educator and you are strong with those traits because it's what you do everyday...I am living in the world as an artist...it is what I do everyday...as you struggle with the artist inside you, I struggle with the side of me that needs balance and structure and organization, common sense, etc.

Barbie is right. In the midst of my career as an educator, my daily struggle is to provide room for the artist to explore and flourish. She, on the other hand, functions as a career artist with her thriving floral business. As a result, the practical is often the most difficult for her to implement. Nevertheless, I believe the profound and the practical can walk hand in hand to temper both our creative and our responsible sides. The result is sweet serenity. This is especially true for the artist/educator.

I recently ordered a light box my sister showed me. (When a creative resource comes across my path, I purchase without hesitation.) This wonderful tool came only a couple of days ago and the drawings I have made since now litter my living room. I created my first light box sketch from a vivid photograph of a rose in my garden. I drew the picture with charcoal paper creating a ruddy appearance. Then, I sketched using drawing paper and a black prism pencil. The light box helped me see an image as shapes and shadows as I followed the pattern so clearly visible. It is as if you directly access the artistic part of the brain without the cognitive pressure to scale an object into realistic proportions. Switching the light source off reveals the image's dark and light shadows and boldly outlined form. The effect is mesmerizing.

Whenever I discover new creative tools like this, I think past myself to how I can share them with students, teachers, and friends. This must come from the combined artist and educator in me. I pass on these novel discoveries to my own two artistic daughters as well. Before school ended, I brought my light box into the classroom and watched as students enjoyed tracing objects.

As someone who has had to manage these two streams of gifting, artist and educator, I have noted some interesting observations. An artist draws away into his or her creative space in order to flesh out imagination's forms through art mediums. The artist/educator emerges from this space with a passion for passing on the craft. He or she finds ways to break down the process into easy-to-follow steps for others. The link between that quiet place of creativity and the pubic sphere of influence marks the unique profile of the artist/teacher.

How tragic that so many artistic educators languish due to working in public schools. The current budget crisis has nailed the coffin of "no art" completely shut. Art in school was already dying, but now we teachers fear reprisals from straying too far from the adopted curriculum. When I am robbed of fulfilling this duplicity of passion and purpose, a marked frustration develops. I have heard these frustrations expressed so many times by teachers who are artistically gifted. The unrest of spirit and dissatisfaction with the job can remain undefined for years until the artist/educator stumbles upon a unique discovery—he or she desperately needs time alone to process feelings and to create. Time away from the demands of career, in order to pursue quiet contemplation, is healing to the spirit and ignites the talents.

The process is much like a cocooned caterpillar. A chrysalis of seclusion forms as you focus on your artistic passions without the frenzy of the classroom and school. Much needed repose begins the process of transformation as your innate gifting sprouts like wings from a back hunched in mental and emotional exhaustion. In time, creative wings emerge, allowing the artistic educator to take flight over the often dry, mandated curriculum required in current classrooms. You re-enter the classroom refreshed and hopeful. You also discover innovative ways to enhance the curriculum without straying from the content.

Lately, I have noticed the detriments of the driven nature of the educational system with its massive gears that chew up spontaneity, openness, and creativity. It is a career fraught with endless "have to" lists that keep teachers and administrators running from one activity or meeting to another. It often fosters relationships only to facilitate the "checking off" of one more burdensome task. It creates a world of rushed conversations that leaves little time for asking, "How are you?" let alone "What is your passion?" Sound familiar? I'm sure the world of education is not the only one filled with symptoms that are so toxic to creativity.

At a recent meeting with colleagues and a district administrator, I saw a teacher that I'd worked with to form a writers' support group. Unhindered by time, our group met outside of school in order to share our passion, discuss publishing, and plan creative lessons. I asked her how her personal writing was going. Her face glowed as she quickly responded, "I have another piece completed. It's so therapeutic." Our personal conversation halted as the others entered the room. The meeting began and clipped along at a steady pace until the agenda items were accomplished. I grieved inside, wanting to linger with my writing friend to discuss our shared passion.

I thought it odd that we educators, who are expected to teach writing, do not take more time to discuss our passions and processes of writing. Instead, we teach a highly academic, and limited, writing style in essay form, which is necessary for passing the state writing exam. These prescriptive essays may prepare for school success, but they fall miserably short in developing students' passion for finding and using their personal voice.

I left the meeting saddened by a system that barely scratches the surface of writing's many delightful expressions. I walked to my car after that meeting feeling deeply troubled for today's youth and a question interrupted my thoughts. "If I only have a certain amount of time on this earth with which to live, create, and inspire, how can I best spend these moments?" This morning as I write, ideas come to mind on how I might provide student-friendly, artistic resources online. I brainstormed ideas on how to capture the artistic gifts of others and invite eager youth to explore various artistic endeavors. Together we can learn to create and write. We can dare to dream our seemingly impossible dreams or capture the fleeting pictures of our imaginations. Most importantly, I will take the time to ask, "How are you?" and "What is your passion?"

EMBRACING MULTIPLE MANTLES

Part of the secret of success in pursuing art is to learn to live with the inherent tension between various inner gifts and external realities. The key is to find a way to live with and manage that natural tension.

I need to write and create as I need to breathe. I welcome those interludes without teaching in order to indulge my writer. In contrast to the sequential, language-based pursuits of teaching, my inner artist favors the part of my brain that is creative and quite opposed to my customary overworking mode. Creating a piece of art takes me away from cerebral overload and brings a soothing and relaxing release. I understand this mystery when I watch my two artist daughters as they "go into the zone," laying out their art supplies—paints, pencils, charcoal. They begin moving from a core deep inside of their souls. Hours often pass with annoying interruptions that momentarily jolt repose. From the time my daughter was a small child, Elya would disappear into her room for hours in order to create. I often poked my head in to check on her, only to find a blissful child in a world of her own design.

Perhaps I can learn from her artistic tendency to move with creativity. Allowing my inner artist to enjoy unhindered exploration is necessary in order to manage these mantles of educator, writer, and artist. I must regularly stop and rest under shady trees of early mornings, uninterrupted weekends, and time-rich holidays by sliding the educator mantle to the ground and picking up my pen. Writing is necessary because it feeds my soul while sculpting, floral design, sketching, gardening, or crocheting bring refreshment from the weariness of the workplace.

My inner artist is quite like a temperamental child, refusing to rush through play and reveling in long spans of time to create. Often my writing and art intertwine. One writing weekend, I explored self-actualization as the emergence from a cocoon of longing. Four sketches resulted that fully consumed the weekend. I did not sketch again for quite some time. Only after allowing my writer and artist full reign for a season can I pull the heavy cloak of teaching over my shoulders once again.

Taking the time to sort through these complexities of purpose serves the creative educator well. Often I err when I assume that because I love it all, all must equally deserve my time, but this is not necessarily true. Frankly, there are not enough moments in the day to do everything. Each pursuit seems to have a season of expression. For instance, I love to dance and to choreograph and I have pursued this as an essential part of a former career; however, my body, now past its prime, enjoys co-leading a middle school's ballroom dance group with one of my daughters. We take every chance we can get to dance together, whether with a band on vacation or through the aisles of a store to music.

Just before Christmas break is my favorite time to teach students dough sculpturing. Flour-padded hands mold a simple mixture of flour, salt, and water as students go into "the artistic zone." Even the rowdy and rambunctious become sedate as they delight in forming their own masterpieces. These youth desperately need to create. They live in a fast-paced, tech-driven society in which social networking keeps them continually connected. Creativity calms their souls and allows their minds to rest. Creating rejuvenates their spirits and improves an overall sense of well being, from which all students benefit.

Every year I begin exposing my students to the glorious soul food of writing. Just ten minutes at the start of class propels many to take the craft up at home. I find them returning with journals packed full of musings. One precocious teen said, "Mrs. Luna, I don't know what you're doing to me but all I want to do is write poetry and stories."

Over the course of the year, the journals help students to deal with their anger. I offer the option of placing a sticky note on the page they would like me to read. I often jot a few thoughts on their journal pages in response.

As we read and share together, I notice a change. Angry tempers begin to disintegrate, resulting in social harmony. Sometimes groups of students will ask to come in during lunch time to discuss relational issues that surface while they journal.

Once a former student's mother came up to me in a restaurant.

"Mrs. Luna, my son is now in high school and writes poetry. He told me that he feels terrible for making fun of your poetry when he was in your class in the 7th grade. Recently, he called me and asked, 'Mom, can you bring me my books of poetry?' He's reading his poetry to the other students and it has helped him to express his emotions."

We stop once a month for an art project, putting our academic left-brains aside. This bonds us together and to our inner artists. Each week we have project learning time for digital design. Students write their own books, work on personal photo stories, and construct their "I Can Change my World" PowerPoint projects. Having the lowest literacy students from grades 6 to 8 tests my patience and endurance. Yet in some mysterious way, writing and creativity helps students shoulder their own heavy mantles of education.

After returning to my classroom from a luscious three-week holiday break, chipper faces waited to tell their tales.

"I didn't get a Christmas present."

"I was bored."

"I live at a Motel 6."

"Mrs. Luna, I wrote all during the break."

"I did too."

The chorus of voices chirped, welcoming the day. Once again, I know why I manage multiple mantles, one as an educator, one as a writer, and one as an artist.

Perhaps my artist and educator identities may eventually reach a compromise of balance, neither reigning solely nor exerting power over the other. This is the essence of my envisioned balance. Unfortunately, I think not. Each vies and volleys for position and control, winning at different junctures of my life, yet all the while propelling me forward in pursuit of my unique destiny.

The artist ignites the fire of passion for life while the educator guides and monitors the movement. The artist resents restraint while the educator spurns lack of control, and each pushes and pulls for dominance. New horizons eventually replace my fantasies of balance, and I find I may never fully master integration of such complex personality traits.

Yet the tension remains and in its midst, I walk daily. Concern over which opportunities to pursue and which to pass by drains my mental energy. Often, my artist calls to abandon its present career path with tantalizing mirages of business pursuits. These off-task bird walks riddle my path. *Should I create a subscription-based technology site?* Once I'm engrossed in a pursuit, the inner artist grows weary of the grind and becomes like a spoilt child demanding freedom. Off she prances into some other fantasy leaving the educator sorting through files of work in search of some obvious ribbon of destiny to grasp and follow. Yes, I was able to create a plethora of digital resources for the benefit of teachers and students, but my temperamental artist rarely rests long enough to enjoy the fruit of my labor. Conversely, she grumbles over the limited progress of the next website, which centers on a creativity theme.

Perhaps the conflict between my inner artist and educator is much like sibling rivalry. Having a sister of my own, I understand this productive tension. As educators and artists, my sister and I balance each other's extremes and prod each other forward. Her inner educator follows me into technology pursuits; my inner artist follows her into writing and art. Recently, she showed me a sketch inspired by a new art book she bought and my heart sang with delight. I will order the book today! We coach each other to resist the vortex of educational needs that sucks the very life right out of our souls. We exhort each other to persist in creating space around our minds and in our lives to allow the artists inside to play unabashedly. Without my sister, I would surely have perished in some doctoral program or office, writing another school plan for an overworked principal.

Just as my earthly sister brings balance to my educator and artist, I must allow those portions of who I am to war against each other until a peaceful ceasefire is achieved. Progress is actually found in the struggle between competing desires and in the relinquishment of preconceived ideas on how the creative life should look.

SHAPING ONE'S CREATIVE PATH

Moving forward with your creativity does necessitate regular reflection in order to sift and sort through new options. Once I master skills, new possibilities present themselves. Setting new priorities for our limited time proves as difficult as learning the needed skills in the first place. One must project into the future in order to envision all that it takes to carry out the proposed idea. Envisioning your new pursuit or idea against the backdrop of life's practical demands helps you to decide if it is something worthy of your time.

It is a warm and wind-hushed Sunday morning in May. A discussion between my husband and I about future direction waylaid my usual early morning writing time. We explored ideas for expanding my educational website to include animated learning games, an idea that would employ writing skills, educational expertise, and digital design skills. We talk about what it would take to create interactive games as an engaging avenue for learning. I wonder what it would take to maintain my core value of innovational freedom of expression. Without this baseline, I quickly feel trapped and frustrated.

I would have to expand my repertoire of technology skills to include creating 3-d cartoon animation. Summer weeks of freedom provide a limited amount of time for finishing the first two manuscripts that are already a priority, so if I am to learn a new technical skill, I will have to set realistic learning goals for the following year.

As my husband and I discussed these ideas, I felt the all too familiar heart tug between my two passions: education and writing. I wonder how long I can maintain this course of parallel growth. As more technology skills amass, more opportunities open. Sorting through what I can do and want to do is precarious. I enjoy my current freedom and fear enslavement to a business.

Mixed into this mental quandary is my desire to remain true to my sense of destiny. Mine seems twofold: integrating literacy, technology, and the arts into learning enhancers and writing for human inspiration. Both compete for limited mental energy and free time. If I am hard-pressed to place one higher on the priority list than the other, I could not choose. My career in education consumes the workweek while writing requires early mornings, afternoons, evenings, and most weekends. Adding the time to master animation and game software would fill my summer days more than I can presently handle. In the end, I decide to postpone new learning until I finish my manuscripts. I must also make time for vacationing with precious family and friends.

Recently a colleague asked me, "When do you sleep?"

I cringed. If only she knew all that I do, she would think me neurotic! Yet the tree of creativity proves fruitful when the conscientious gardener learns how to prune for productivity. Your destiny grows from a strong root system that develops over a lifetime. The technology, education, and writing expertise I have mastered resulted from years of devotion to learning and practicing. Time and effort expanded the trunk. Branches emerged as I explored gifts and interests. Now the time for pruning is at hand. I must continually ask myself, "Which branches do I wish to keep and which do I prune into more fruitful boughs?" I sacrificed some in order to redirect limited resources. These decisions are complex and arduous. Only through reflective writing, devoted intercession, and ongoing discussions with others can I ever hope to make the wisest choices most aligned with my core values.

Cultivating creativity has taught me many lessons. One is that our lives grow over time—just as a mighty tree begins its journey from a seedling and grows to a sapling, an innovator begins by following those things that ignite excitement in his or her soul. Every new pursuit requires a season of skill mastery. As in nature, winter allows time for root formation and expansion. During these times, not a lot of productivity seems possible. Then spring brings blossoms that eventually become fruit ripe for the picking. The wise creator embraces times for developing skills as wholeheartedly as times for building products.

Each one of us enjoys God-given talents and the privilege of working in tandem with the Master of all Creativity in developing the gifts He has bestowed. Whatever shape our tree takes depends upon human collaboration with divine artistry. I long to enter my golden years as a sun-kissed gardener who faithfully labored towards a destiny that changes lives. I long to let the seasons flow as God opens my eyes to the possibilities. I purpose my heart, mind, and soul to remain sensitive to His directions and to welcome His disciplines as he shapes my creative destiny.

A wise old woman once sat under the shade of a fruitful tree while resting from her labor. With a basket full of fruit nestled under her arm she mused, "I will take this harvest to hungry children in the village below." While leaning against the ruddy trunk—now wide enough to hold her fragile frame—she pondered the lengthy growth process necessary for such a blessing for humankind to emerge.

"How many seasons has this tree withstood the tests of time?" she mused.

She also knew all too well how rigorous her pruning had been as she sought to form this wonder of nature into a tree that could reach its full capacity.

Then stopping to reflect upon her life, she determined to be like the tree. "I will welcome the Gardener of my Soul to prune and shape until finding my most fruitful form!"

Then the woman arose and faithfully carried the basket of fruit towards the village below.

EXERCISE

Identify an earthly season that best describes your present creative season. If it is spring, do you have the desire to clean out, organize, and then plant new ideas or activities? Are you in summer, resting on your laurels and awaiting the harvest? Is it fall and time for harvesting some of your hard work? Has winter descended? Do you desire the life of a recluse so you can go deeper with your writing? Perhaps you long to create in isolation. Write about your conclusions and then rest in your present process.

CHAPTER 8

MANAGING CREATIVITY

"Every child is an artist. The problem is how to
remain an artist once he grows up."
-Pablo Picasso

THE GLORIOUS MUSE WE WRITE TO...

Muse: A mysterious and sometimes mystical source that ignites our imagination and inspires our writing or other creative ventures (JoDee's definition). I never cease to be amazed at the sources of inspiration that come along unexpectedly. These sparks of innovation drift into my mind both day and night. I have learned to train myself to stop, listen, and record these fleeting ideas. The act of writing returns—in words—this inspiration to the glorious muse we write to...

So what ignites my imagination? One chapter is not long enough to list all of my sources for inspiration, but I'll share a few here, along with some ideas on how to learn to listen to your muse.

As a very visual person, images tend to serve as one of my muses. My favorite writing spot has a large window from which I can see our backyard. The colorful greens, pinks, and reds of plants and blooms stir my creative juices.

Throughout the day and night, I try to stop and focus on a scene or object that intrigues me. This may be something beautiful to my eyes or an occurrence that moves me because of the tragedy involved. Life presents muses if we train ourselves to capture their essence and use them as inspiration. Here are a few helpful hints on how to capture the thoughts your muses will generate:

1. Be ready at all times! I keep a three-ring binder on my nightstand along with a pen and my cell phone. The cell phone provides a light source. Disciplining myself to roll over and write ideas down was not an easy process. Everything in the fiber of my body rejects this practice even to this day, but I do it anyway. The notebook stays in my car during the day, and I carry a small pad and mini tape recorder in my purse as well. Often I receive songs while driving to work and record them in the parking lot.

2. Train yourself to ponder. If you awaken in the night from a dream, do not rush rising. Lay still and silent in case your muse generates images, words, or ideas. Record them quickly or they will float away on butterfly wings.

3. Keep a camera handy. My favorite photo shoot times are early in the morning when the air stills and the sun first kisses my roses. The natural lighting is spectacular.

I also love the late afternoon right before sunset. The natural lighting glows with a slight amber hue. I have a great window spot to set up a quick photo shoot during this time of the day.

My expensive Canon XTI Rebel digital camera comes with me on planned photography excursions, but I also keep a cheaper and smaller digital camera in the car for impromptu pictures that present. Recently, I forgot my camera, and while driving to work, a huge rainbow-colored hot air balloon rose before me. I fumed and fussed over missing that amazing picture. Photos often inspire my blog posts with their interesting lighting, colors, images, and scenes.

4. Weed out those things that dampen your muse. Dysfunctional living is a sure way to kill your muse. The temptation to live in other people's drama saps your creative strength. Drama feeds off creative resources so make sure the recent "crisis" does not rob yours. Until I began weeding out drama, I could not move forward successfully with hint #5.

5. Set aside "my time" to explore different forms of creativity that ignite inspiration for writing. The demands of everyday life will squeeze the muses from your life if you don't set aside time for yourself to create. Different artists and writers I've spoken to explain their best creative times, which often differ from mine; however, one thing is a constant. These amazing people value themselves enough to set aside time to create. This was perhaps the single most difficult discipline I had to learn to implement. Codependents constantly focus on the needs of others and find it difficult to nurture their own creativity. The high received from helping is our drug of choice.

6. Search for your "tribe" as author Ken Robinson describes in his book *The Element*. Creativity begets creativity and like-minded people will serve as muses for one another. Find the people who love what you love. This is by far one of my greatest joys and the reason I blog. I have met amazing artists, writers, and musicians who ignite my love of creativity. I have even ventured into art forms

foreign to me by visiting the blogs of artists and writers. This summer's exploration into mixed media art had its inception in tribe searching.

7. Create a vision you can grow into. Sure, it will change but set your goal high enough that you can reach towards expansion. I imagine being a creativity coach someday, but I would be thrilled over a few people finding their muse through my blog sites.

Managing the Creative Flow

This morning I awoke thinking about managing creativity. Creative energy flows through human regulators much like water through a nozzle on the end of a hose. At first, the inexperienced delight in learning how to turn on the flow, which ends up with creativity going everywhere and soaking everything without directed purpose. In time, creative eclectics learn wisdom concerning creative flow and regulation.

This analogy is fresh in my mind from last evening's gardening. Often I like to water without a nozzle because the flow is softer on the plants and flowers; however, in between pots, the water goes everywhere. After dousing our patio plants, the cement, and me, the surroundings looked more like the kids had enjoyed a water fight than that I had watered. I like to create in much the same way. Once the ideas start, I enjoy an unobstructed flow that pours into various projects, but after a few hours I am exhausted because my mind cannot contain the inundation of ideas for an extended period. If I do not stop to take regular brain breaks, ideas eventually dissipate into the spilled waters of my mind.

Creativity management is essential when working on extensive projects or developing new talents. Yes, innate abilities are often traceable to childhood. The "bent" is there and the first step is learning to let it flow yet regulation is a key component in developing gifting or the constant flow can exhaust. Part of managing innovation is recognizing and heeding the symptoms of creative overload.

My inner artist does not like the nozzle because pacing is a challenge for the creative eclectic. Often, in the midst of furiously working on a project, one feels overwhelmed and annoyed. This signals the need to put the project down for a while. During these "off times," other currents draw us into other pursuits. I have learned to make allowances for rest. Rest refuels the soul and empowers a return to writing. When I become irritated while working on a project, I have learned to walk away. Doing other activities reenergizes my mind.

My driven self balks when I break from a manuscript in order to refuel with a brief walk. Yet if I continue to push myself and do not take regular breaks, I eventually collapse into a heap of exhaustion and discouragement. The mind can only generate ideas for so long before rest is in order. When I feel those symptoms of burnout coming on after hours of intense concentration on a project, I often do some mindless tasks. For instance, on those Saturdays that I spend writing manuscripts, every so often I will look for a household chore to complete: straightening rooms, folding clothes, putting away dishes, or organizing closets. It's a great way to get household chores done in bite-size pieces while also refreshing your mind. I can always tell when I need a break because I start to feel physically agitated and restless. The stretch break does wonders for releasing physical and mental tension.

Today I will exit my home on this glorious Dr. Martin Luther King Jr. Day and run a few errands that will lighten my upcoming week's demands. Oh, make no mistake. The inner artist screams to buy more yarn for crocheting, and I will appease this request. I may even linger over some piece of artwork as I did while photographing this morning's sunrise. However, the main purpose of this outside venture will be to pull myself away from the project at hand. Breaking my concentration is essential in order to return with a fresh perspective.

I find that I can extend my creative productivity using this intermittent distraction method; yet, after some hours, I eventually hit the wall. When this happens, no amount of distracting can pull me back into the project. I am done for the day, ready to stop. I have learned from experience that pushing past this point always proves counterproductive.

I become quite sullen if I don't regulate creative flow. Even the artistic project becomes all work and no play, for the artist inside is like a willful child who has not yet learned the benefits of healthy self-care. She wants to empty the flow of every droplet, instead of pacing herself in order to channel the flow over time. Can you really blame the childlike trait that finds creativity so irresistible? When waters of ideas move, it is so tantalizing to jump onto a raft and ride the playful rapids; however, one only has to go over the falls of overindulgence a few times to learn that prudence is essential. Take the time to rest from creating and eventually you will learn how to manage the creative flow.

HELPFUL HINTS FOR GOAL SETTING

How do eclectic creative people set goals when the very nature of this personality type delights in daily spontaneity? For this creative eclectic, goal setting must intersperse with intermittent free play. My son's business advice regularly includes writing a business plan. He says that I must decide where I want to be in the future and then lay out the process in achievable steps. My life experience, though, readily acknowledges inclusion of both goal setting and unrestricted free play. Many times, I have followed a plan; yet, my creative nature resists attempts to harness and tends toward spontaneity. I have also discovered that God's intentions for my destiny often remain veiled until I pursue the things that bring me joy.

The pursuit of an educational career necessitated goal setting in order to acquire a Bachelor of Arts, Multiple Subject Teaching Credential, and Master of Arts in Education. Each degree necessitated evaluating the final goal then setting the steps into place to reach it. I finished three degrees over an eight-year period, walking through the requirements one at a time. The creative child in me was duly harnessed for very long periods, free only for brief interludes during school breaks. Becoming a professional development trainer allowed a bit more play as opportunities arose unexpectedly to create unique classes for teachers.

Eventually, my creative self willfully demanded expression after years of career structure. Ideas bubbled up through desert terrain, like oil through the earth's surface. Yet, for my childlike heart, the mere existence of oil was not reason enough to drill further. My creative heart was a fickle, gypsy spirit, sweeping from one pursuit to another. Sometimes I just liked to do what I desired that day instead of working towards another goal.

After those restrictive years of career building, I had to enjoy a season of lavish creating. One moment, scrapbooking delighted me, resulting in five photo albums that became Christmas gifts for the family. The next Christmas, the thought of making one for myself appealed to me about as much as being boiled in oil. Play that becomes obsessive tends to characterize the creative eclectic and when the fun stops, motivation bumps into the halted pied piper. Creative pursuits can fascinate just like a toy that possesses the heart of a child for hours, until he glibly tosses it aside. Some other pursuit captures the imagination and the present project is abandoned.

Our artistic sides need room to breathe and design at whim. One of my present fantasies involves finding a business manager who could take my artwork to the market. How wonderful to partner with someone whose sole objectives are the practical components that I despise. Until this mystery person manifests, though, I will allow my creative child full reign to run out and stomp in puddles of the imagination.

Eventually, the desire to play led me to make long-term goals in order to achieve a product. For instance, I decided to put my writings together into books, build websites to house ideas about education and creativity, and advance my artwork. I found that goals are necessary in order to channel exploration into tangible projects.

The first priority I set into place after implementing regular writing times was to analyze my schedule in order to partition off project time. I am the freshest in the morning, so I decided to get up earlier with my husband at 4:45am before work. I began working on long-term projects after my usual writing. Then I decided to take the first few hours of the weekend mornings as well. Afternoons and evenings served as time to type my journal writings into computer files and take web-design lessons. Eventually, my writing capacity grew, and I found myself writing for longer periods.

Over time, my writing goals expanded to include pacing throughout the year. I estimated the amount of pages I could complete in a week and then multiplied this figure to get an idea of how long it would take to finish my first manuscript. The next step was to develop a template for keeping track of my books and page counts. This visual reminder helped me to develop realistic timeframes. Then I began to research the world of publishing, learning the steps of what to do next.

After I accomplished my goal of adding long-term project time to writing time, I decided to do the same for art integration. When I have a holiday break from teaching, I take the time to indulge my artistic side with various arts and craft projects.

Certain seasons of the year seem the right fit for different art forms. For instance, I enjoy salt dough sculpting of ornaments during the fall and Christmas season and floral design during spring and summer. Sketching is an enjoyable art form, which I do throughout the year.

Even though setting long-term goals is necessary, I must make allowances for creativity to develop freely once again. Whenever an artistic delight becomes something I feel I must do, I step back and reevaluate my goals and objectives. Life is far too short for any more projects that make me feel trapped. Set goals, but leave enough free space for your artistic side to explore.

MULTIPLE PROJECT MANAGEMENT

"I am the gentle gardener watering your visions in the night."

Last night I awoke from a dream in which the Lord was counseling me about focus. He explained that the visions He has given me are like flowers in my garden. Some are to be contained and some transplanted into larger containers. However, some will climb over the garden wall in order to spread seeds in other places. All are to grow simultaneously.

This concept of moving multiple projects forward defies a linear approach, but perhaps it coincides with the artistic mind. In the midst of my confusion, serenity comes from knowing that God sees the larger picture. In retrospect, the talents I've cultivated in my life needed to grow all at the same time, though they have expanded at different rates. For instance, if I had not learned web design while creating innovative trainings, I would not have an educational technology website to serve the teachers and students attending my classes. Writing my various book manuscripts provided timely words of encouragement for friends and family.

"For it is the Spirit who gives life; the flesh profits nothing; the words I speak are Spirit and Life" (John 6:63). Following the Spirit of God is unpredictable. No human can control this process (though we all try vehemently to do so). This understanding brings acceptance of how God has wired our creative being. We must shed all remnants of shame because each of us is unique. We must no longer slink before the linear thinkers who produce best by lining up their project into neat steps. We must dare to discover the plans of God as He decides, discerning which to prune and which to expand. Surely, we will not follow perfectly, but to live any other way seems like death for the creative soul.

With this said, I do believe there is a place for managing multiple projects. Part of being a good steward of the talents God has bestowed requires mastery of this skill in whatever form works for you. I envision the year as a running track with an oblong shape. I even create this picture in digital form in a computerized word document. The winter and summer are the long stretches while the spring and fall form the bending curves. I note projects by placing them along the track, and if more than one is in process, I prioritize which will receive most of my time by placing it on top. For example, this summer's priority is to finish my manuscript. The pencil editing took place early in the summer as I scribbled corrections onto a printed copy in a three-ring binder. Now summer speeds by as I enter those corrections digitally before returning to work.

Mentally I must purpose to delay other desired projects until I achieve this objective. Working on my blog and creativity site will have to wait. Once the manuscript is completed, I can allow time to pursue the other projects. I do occasionally indulge in the desire to take creative bird walks; however, the main project of focus is at the forefront of my mind every single day I create. Finishing projects in this way allows me to enjoy the fruit of my labor and brings me a sense of accomplishment.

Managing multiple projects simultaneously is difficult but doable if you learn to think on multiple tracks. Imagine a course that aligns with your year and set your goals flexibly enough to push back estimated timelines if needed. The race should be enjoyable and not forced in order for the creativity to keep flowing. The years will go by whether or not you finish that painting or write that book. Wouldn't it be nice to eventually hold something you have made in your hand?

Another important skill to move projects forward is to adjust timeframes as needed. We creative eclectics tend to plan far more than possible in any twenty-four hour period. As a result, we need to readjust our expectations on a regular basis to find what is realistic. This takes practice but it is very possible.

For example, my educational-technology website venture proved more time consuming than previously anticipated; just making basic changes siphoned away many evenings and weekend hours. I now chuckle at how naïve I was in thinking I could design a website in only a couple of months. I naively tossed ideas around in ignorance as to the time each endeavor would require. Yet in spite of reassessing and narrowing my focuses, developing an additional website for my first book has become irresistible. Involvement in these two projects has made me aware of how we eclectics must be realistic about our timeframes. We will rarely focus on just one project, so finishing anything always takes longer than we planned. There is nothing wrong with lengthening our projected finish date if need be.

I continue learning to adjust my expectations and lengthen my timelines. As the anonymous quote so wisely asserts, "There are no unrealistic goals, just unrealistic timeframes." The amount of time I calculate for finishing projects is typically far too short-sided. I always seem to underestimate what I can complete in any given day.

Finishing my first book took about a year longer than I had planned. My editing and revising time multiplied into three rewrites, instead of the one I planned. Finding a professional editor who matches my writing genre has not been easy. Now I understand why some authors talk about their books like a marriage of sorts. Years can pass while you pour countless hours, days, and months into a project. Add to this all of the other interests people like us have. I am finally coming to accept that pushing back my timeframes is just a part of this process. With age, you do learn to know yourself a bit more, and you get better at setting realistic goals.

Meanwhile, trying to balance a demanding career and multiple outside projects proves energizing. I have finally accepted my innate desire for diverse challenges. I am just not a "one-project-at-a-time" type of person. I choose to develop multiple areas, knowing that the attention and devotion required often result in unfinished works. Perhaps this mode of operating will slow down or entirely prevent the completion of any one "great work," but for me to live otherwise does not appeal.

I have finally settled the multi-faceted issue. Maybe this is because I realize how truly short life is. I want to squeeze every moment out of the days left. I embrace all aspects of my makeup, including these somewhat fragmented tendencies that frustrate me at times.

A phone call interrupts this writing. My multi-talented mother excitedly reports twelve inches of snow, her photo shoot to capture the beauty, and plans to develop digital newsletters on the new touch screen computer she recently purchased. Is it any wonder I am who I am?

STREAMLINING FOR PRODUCTIVITY: PARTITIONING YOUR CREATIVE SELF

As I reenter another educational work year, a panic settles in as to how I can retain my creative development while the vortex of my job sucks me into an intense work environment. Every year

I promise the little girl of mirth inside my soul that I will protect her light-hearted candor and innovative knack. This year I will partition my creative self in order to fulfill this promise. I will accept and celebrate my many sides versus forcing them together.

Here is how it works. Several years ago I bought a dual 160-gig hard drive computer. I partitioned each 80-gig hard drive for a certain purpose. Drive C contained certain programs pertaining to my career as an educator. It also housed files and folders of compiled work pertaining to education. In contrast, drive D was the creative holding tank. This housed Adobe Creative Suite CS3 software along with my websites, writings, designs, artwork, and photography.

With these partitions and organizational systems, I could create, develop, and save in the appropriate files. I could always detect where my passions ebbed and flowed depending upon the enlargement of files and multiplication of folders. For instance, this summer was a season of advancing book projects as reflected by a growing abundance of word documents. I also worked extensively on my websites and the growth of images and resources expanded.

Just as I did with my computer, my hope is to protect and save this creative flow as I start the work year by partitioning off my creative self. I try to separate work from home as much as possible. When I am at work, I give myself completely to the task; however, when I am home, it is my time. The very nature of a demanding career is that it sucks the life out of the artistic soul. Therefore, I am careful to protect my free time.

When I am at home, I balance freely creating with purposeful "Project Time." Project Time is when I take the raw materials of journal entrees, photography, or artwork and nearly create a work. I say "nearly" because no project ever seems fully completed to an innovator. Project Time may include digitizing writing from journal into computer or designing web pages. It requires both sides of the brain: my creative right and logical left. The emergence of projects also requires critical analysis in order to fashion something new. Project Time is most enjoyable if I have lots of uninterrupted time. I go into my creative zone and emerge hours later, wondering where the time went.

Even though a teacher's schedule lends itself to blocks of time off, I have learned the necessity of including another essential partition in order to avoid burn out—time for refreshment. Working extensively on creative endeavors drains the mind of ideas and the soul of emotions. Artistic people live in their minds and souls and they reflect to the world the wrestling, perception, and beauty others seldom explore.

I first noticed a pattern of daily depression descending after an extended project time. I rode the waves of creativity for several hours until they crashed onto the sands of my soul. Exhausted mentally and emotionally, I wondered about these odd moods, which were quite apparent when creating day after day during a summer break. Then I started breaking these dismal moods with a walk through my gardens or around the block. The negativity started to lift, so the excursions expanded outside the confines of home to trips through garden sections of local stores. Flowers and foliage seem to ground me in appreciating God's natural beauty. Another enjoyable outing is walking through an arts and crafts store admiring other's creativity.

Refreshment is unique to each one of us. What instills new life in you may be quite different from what I enjoy. Working alone can starve your soul of companionship, so a quick phone call to a family member or friend often does the trick. On desperate occasions, I link up with someone near and dear, like my sister, for a coffee and chat. Times of refreshment must be uncensored. Just yesterday, I witnessed this in real life when a small boy spied a model train in a display window. He glanced longingly at his mother with pleading eyes saying, "Look!"

She lovingly returned, "We must stop and look at this!"

Could we not learn to be as loving with our creative selves who long for time away from life's demands? Yes, there is a time for mainstream work, whatever that may be for each one of us. However, partitioning additional times for reflection, project work, and refreshment will propel us forward on this path of creativity while preserving the child-like temperament and artistic innovator within.

THE FINE ART OF PLATE TWIRLING

Have you ever felt like one of those plate twirlers at the circus? You know the trick: you get one plate spinning and then add another one until several are moving simultaneously. This is often the way us creative eclectics approach life. We cannot resist just one more interesting project, so we hoist it up in the air on top of another stick. Unfortunately, limited time and experience inevitably cause some of our ingenious creations to come crashing down. We lose perspective and have to pick up the pieces once again.

I have practiced the fine art of plate twirling over an entire lifetime. My brilliant teacher, Mom, twirled multiple interests and taught my sister and me to do the same. So in reminiscing the "how to's" of this art form, I have come up with some helpful hints:

1. Accept mediocrity. Ouch! That will not go down well with those creative eclectic perfectionists out there, but hear me out before you respond. The very nature of multiple twirling means you have to be gentle with yourself when the product is substandard according to your critical assessment. Maintain a playful attitude—at least for some creative endeavors. Over time, it will become clearer which endeavors need your inner "grown up" to kick in with some discipline.

2. Know when to toss a dish (project) aside. Often what we start ends up not as we intended. For example, my daughter Andy and I recently decided to take a break from a five-year commitment of co-leading one of my school's performing arts groups. A decline in commitment from the youth began to wear us down and we started dreading the practices. One day I heard one excuse too many and said, "That's enough!" Remember the importance of play. See Hint #10.

3. Although it's ok to be a creative coach potato occasionally, try to get up and pursue something you think you might enjoy. Every time I watch "Dancing with the Stars" or "So you Think you Can Dance?" I get starry-eyed and want to dance again. Recently, Andy recruited me for a jazz/swing dance and we have been rehearsing. Yikes! I get winded easily, teeter due to my equilibrium being off, and cannot get past looking at my fat thighs in the dance studio mirror. This experience is helping me to have more realistic dance expectations. Yet even though the rehearsals prove challenging, I'm proud of myself for having at least tried.

4. Only twirl what you cannot imagine living without. Although I pine over dozens of artistic delights, I cannot live without writing, blogging, photography, photo editing, and sketching. These are the main plates I will always keep spinning.

5. Just because a plate falls and breaks into pieces doesn't mean that you shouldn't gather those pieces and glue them together. My first book about creativity meets this criterion. My sister, Gina, and I are in the process of a major overhaul edit, slash, and reorganize. I doubt the finished product will look anything like the original.

6. Create a lifestyle model of plate twirling that works for you. Each of us has unique life demands that necessitate being flexible. I try to figure out how to fit all of my loves into a twenty-four hour period (and still sleep) through a process of trial and error. A lifestyle model slowly formed that works for me. For example, I can write in the morning when refreshed. Editing happens during uninterrupted Saturdays. Evenings are great for photo editing and blogging while enjoying my creative coach potato prerogative. Vacations and long summer breaks lend to art exploration.

7. Accept and defend your tendency to push multiple projects forward. My husband and I go round and round about this. He is convinced I'm not focusing on getting my first book finished with all of the blogging. I see how they fit together and can envision the entire process. He cringes when I talk about starting one more manuscript. I give myself the leeway to have many open-ended projects. Yet, even though my inner artist child enjoys some "free play" time, eventually the grown-up needs to tell that kid to come inside and finish the manuscript!

8. Be selective in sharing your plate twirling. Left-brained, sequential people will think you've lost your mind. In contrast, other right-brained, scattered creative eclectics will encourage you. And balance resides somewhere in the middle of both perspectives.

9. Resist the cultural pulls towards fame and fortune. We live in a worldview dominated by these prerequisites for stamping something worthy.

10. Resist the pressure to perform. As soon as I feel like a project has to be perfect, my interest wanes. I notice that children create

for the very enjoyment of the experience. They do not think, "This has got to be perfect!"

EXERCISE

Take some time to sort through your creative plates. Mentally place them in different categories: those to keep, those to develop, and those to toss. If a plate provokes feelings of dread, it may just be the right time to stop twirling that particular artistic pursuit. You can always pick it up again at a later time.

CHAPTER 9

DISCOVERING YOUR CREATIVE DESTINY

"Destiny begins when you explore who you are, what you want, and where you want to go. Destiny happens when you take those scary steps because you sense God is smiling."
— *JoDee Luna*

THE POWER OF NO REGRETS

There is a power that comes from having no regrets. Passing up opportunities after thoroughly processing and praying leaves the pilgrim free of a lingering "I should have done that" feeling. This insight became apparent recently when I came across an unsent writing submission to a local performing arts production for women. I had labored over whether to send my first monumental writing piece, created while in recovery from the effects of my ex-spouse's sexual addiction and my co-sexual addiction. The piece encapsulates my experiences in a very personal way. I had even designed the cover letter, which left only pressing the send icon on my email. Oddly enough, some reservations within caused me to refrain. The feeling was not fear, for I had processed that emotion. The sensation was not anxiety, for I had also talked through this feeling on paper and with my best friend. The sense was more "You are not ready to go public yet." I then felt an overwhelming desire to save this precious piece for a future book about these life experiences. I admit that after the deadline passed, though, I struggled with whether I had missed an opportunity.

The experience made me wonder how I move past that tortured sense of missed opportunity. Personal experience has taught me that when it comes to exploring a "next best step," start with putting it on paper. Write down all you envision the pursuit will entail then research the possibility further. Find people who have gone down that road and interview them. Take copious notes on insights they have gleaned from their experiences. During this process, imagine yourself walking in their shoes. Note the feelings and thoughts that come to mind as you do.

For instance, when I was contemplating whether to pursue my doctoral degree, I spoke with everyone I could find who had walked through this process. As they shared their reasons for pursuing the PhD, their resulting experiences, and their self-reflections after the fact, it became quite clear to me that the benefits did not outweigh the years and financial costs. I knew I was too old to pursue a tenured position as a university professor and my preferred writing style did not require the credential in order to publish. Therefore, in spite of a colleague's persuasive cajoling to join her in a cohort, I passed up this opportunity without regret.

I faced another fork in the road of destiny when a designer for an educational company requested my resume. As a professional development trainer for my district, I use this company's materials and tout their brilliance. The company was in the process of hiring a California rep, and I was among the candidates. Although they selected someone else with more experience, I endured a suspended period of waiting that forced me to explore whether I would even like the job. It would have required extensive traveling and continual presentations on their materials. As I journaled about the decision, it became quite apparent that I would not have enjoyed the job. My pull toward becoming a published writer required creating a quiet place at home to ponder and produce. I also discovered that I would prefer creating my own professional development courses that integrated literacy, technology, and the arts. Since that time, I have designed many courses for my district, and I had a wonderful opportunity to be a presenter for a Vanguard University series. These opportunities better suited me, and I love every minute of my present lifestyle. Once again, I have no regrets.

The old saying still rings true, "All that glitters is not gold." Instead of searching for the perfect expression for your gifting, try creating it instead. Envision through your morning writings what you would love to do and then begin researching the process steps required. If you venture down a certain path only to discover the fit is disquieting to your soul, then stop and back up to the point where you took the fork in the road.

Paths will often dead-end due to human intervention or lack of it. I have followed more than one business venture to a dismal roadblock due to others not owning the vision. In each situation, I was so sure the opportunity was the right fit only to eventually discover that I was the only one who believed in and worked towards the goal. When this occurs, you have to make a critical decision. Do I continue doing all the work or abandon this pursuit relegating it to another failure? I chose the latter and never looked back with regret. Now I'm convinced that these pursuits would not have suited me in the end. However, these experiences did force me to press into God and to myself in order to discover what would more closely align with my purposes and desires.

Be careful, also, about forcing yourself into unrealistic timeframes for accomplishing your goals. As soon as serenity frazzles into stress, step back and reevaluate. Any pursuit I have engaged that causes consternation has always ended up to be a big fat zero in my life! God moves in paths of peace, and when harmony dissipates, I reassess. Perhaps the direction is right but the timing or season of delivery is forced. Our destinies are complex puzzle pieces that all need to come together, in terms of people, timing, and resources. My daughter often says, "Wait for it." This simple phrase comes to mind whenever I want something NOW! Waiting for God's divine plan proves wise. Jumping ahead too quickly always ends in disappointment.

THE TEST OF SUSTAINABILITY

Just because "you can" does not mean, "you should!" As one develops personal talents and learns new skills, opportunities proliferate like wild flowers in open meadows after spring rains. One merely needs to reach down and pluck bouquets of gifting to display on life's table. However, I have found it most helpful to ask a pertinent question before pursuing an emerging opportunity: "What do I want to sustain?" Often a delectable prospect presents itself, but upon pondering the long-term upkeep, I quickly recoil. I apply the test of sustainability in order to prioritize.

I am a compulsive innovator who thrives on the new and unique. Any ideas that seem right at the onset do not often hold their allure when I imagine having to perform them on a regular basis five years from now. Often I end up with the proverbial "egg on my face" because I decided not to eat what I dished onto my plate. Imagining yourself participating in a given activity in the long-term does weed out impulsivity.

Pressing needs can often color my glasses with a rosy hue. For instance, I was convinced that a side eBay business was the answer to unruly university expenses necessary for my children's educations. I even bought a magazine featuring how to grow an eBay business. I should have gotten a clue from the fact that I never even skimmed through the table of contents. Another opportunity I almost pursued was getting my doctorate. As noted earlier, after taking stock of the costs and sacrifices versus the profitability, my decision wavered like a drunken tightrope walker. The final fall came when I realized I would not enjoy teaching in college.

During these years of searching, an itch continued to annoy me without a sufficient scratch ever hitting the spot. I just knew there was a new branch sprouting from this ole tree trunk, but I could not figure out the form. In time, my passion for writing grew from a mere sapling into a fruitful bow that produced fruit of an unusual kind. This longing eventually transformed from files into actual manuscripts. Other creative pursuits begun at this same time have only grown into small branches, not strong enough to bear significant fruit, which leads me to another principal of sustainability.

Know how to prioritize your passions. When I saw my desire to write growing, as evidenced by journals stacked in my closet and files housed in my computer, I figured the time had come to make finishing manuscripts a priority. This required subduing other artistic impulses during busy career days. Decorating that large wreath for our empty living room wall will have to wait until summer break. Saturdays and Sundays are too sparse for me to justify giving time to decorating versus writing. I set aside this season for writing and force myself to leave the guitar in its case until a few days before bringing it to school per student requests.

When I start to doubt my decision to self-publish, a student brings me a poem written on school-lined paper bearing his vulnerable soul. In the midst of exhortations of "You can become a writer," a tiny voice inside me whispers, "So can you!" I know, once again, that the greater good will come from inspiring youth to write their thoughts and feelings into forms from which others may benefit. This brings me to another test of sustainability: "Does this activity you are considering ignite your sense of destiny or immobilize you with depressing thoughts?" Tracking the things that give you meaning will help you to avoid a misplaced sense of obligation.

Another component of sustainability is to update your personal inventory of "love to's" on a regular basis. These are the activities that you long for and feel energized by doing. For example, my favorite career projects are those that allow me to team with others who have like minds and talents. I am an innovator not an administrator. Knowing this helped me sift through career opportunities selectively instead of ending up regretting or feeling trapped by my commitments.

Ironically, my social enjoyment of creating in tandem or with groups has never materialized in terms of my writing until recently. Most manuscripts are developed solo, without co-authors. Finishing my first two books has meant venturing along the path alone. Although discouraging at times, writing unaccompanied has confirmed to me that I am a writer. This precious assurance proves an invaluable test for sustainability. Although writing can be a lonely craft, I have learned to delight in my own company and to create with my own talents. The experiences I document in the pages of my manuscripts produce an honest journey of someone overcoming seemingly insurmountable odds in order to follow dreams. On a positive note, I have met many writers through blogging and social media, who provide invaluable feedback and encouragement.

Advice from my adult son forever remains etched in my mind. When I was looking for a side venture to pursue, he encouraged me to choose something I would love to do whether or not I ever made money. His advice proved invaluable in following destiny's path. My goal readjusted to binding my writings into book form whether or not they sell as a "hot commodity." I accept the cost of financial outlay without reimbursement. This mindset helps me summon the courage to do this scary thing. Writing as a side interest takes the financial pressure off writing to pay the bills.

One truth is certain, we will all age whether or not we attend the gym, eat healthy food, or pursue heartfelt dreams. Life passes us by at an astounding rate. Ah, but only a few precious pursuits will pass the test of sustainability. May you discover what those are in your lifetime and go after them with all of your heart, mind, soul, and strength.

CREATIVE SOUL SEARCHING

A slight depression settled over me yesterday, mingled with feelings of meaninglessness. I look around at the things people claw and scratch for, and nothing appeals. At work, colleagues grumble over obvious inequities, and I cannot say that I blame them. I try to fly low to the ground, avoiding the radar of criticism. The only desires I have besides advancing my students' literacy and technology proficiency is to ignite their sense of destiny. Aside from this, being a catalyst for creativity within my classes, dance group, and writers' group is the extent of my present ambitions.

When times of reevaluation happen to me, I allow the questions to come and take time to reassess priorities. This is an essential practice for the creative eclectic because we typically feel pulled in so many different directions. As I reflected yesterday, I came to some interesting feelings, thoughts, and conclusions. For example, I have no desire to sit on leadership teams or committees. Decision-making about policies and procedures does not appeal to me in the least. When I look back to a time when being part of a leadership team captivated my heart, I wonder who that person was who has since died and is not seeking resurrection.

What delights my soul is a writer's passion to express thoughts and ponder on the page for eager readers. The desire to express myself through the combination of art, photographs, and writing also intrigues me. The purposeful passion to be a voice to those walking a similar path and wondering, "What's it all about?" seems so right.

Churches, schools, and businesses have their heroes—those who publically speak and sell books, holding a corner of the financial market and the masses' hearts. At one time, I desired to share the limelight of such pursuits but I do not anymore. I merely exist to follow my Lord one day at a time, inspiring hope in another heart and creativity in another soul. Perhaps God is holding me to the promise I wrote in a poem so long ago:

MY QUEST

I never have wanted much glory or fame
Just a heart that was willing to call on your name

And of riches and glory I rarely think twice
When I look to my Savior who paid a dear price

So on earth while I roam all these lonely of days
Lifting eyes up from trouble towards heaven to gaze

I'll surrender my fears that tend to grow wild
To once again trust with the heart of a child

Please help me remember each day that I live
Eternity dwells in the grace that you give

And someday in heaven beside you I'll stand
With pockets so empty and faith that is grand

I have found that resisting cultural definitions of success is essential in order to decide what my priorities will be. Often other creative eclectics help me with this process as I observe their contentment to pursue their divergent art forms. For instance, yesterday I went to my sister's house for a lazy day by her pool. The agenda was lounging and talking. She showed me my birthday present in process and the small 5"x 5" canvas instantly warmed my heart. There was a western-style gate with barbed wire trailing off on both sides. Beyond the gate was unexplored terrain evidenced by no observable path yet worn into the soil. A terracotta flowerpot nestled to the right bottom corner of the fence awaiting vibrant flowers she would soon paint. The earth tones before the fence sprouted with fine yellow grasses and scattered small stones. I wanted to walk right into that picture and stand before that gate.

I saw my sister's eyes dance with delight as she showed me my gift. Her peaceful countenance illuminated her face, and I knew she loved her new little friend so carefully crafted for me in love. Priorities! She set aside time simply to create a gift for a sister she loved…me. Gina teaches me to rest from my ambitious pursuits and enjoy life. This gift will never grace the walls of an art gallery but it will forever alter the priorities of my heart. To love and to be loved are what truly matters.

BEING AT PEACE WITH YOUR PURPOSES

We live in a culture driven by the desire for success as calculated by popularity and wealth. These messages form our value systems as they stream through television and computer screens. While some climb up to the top of the dog pile and wave the flag of success, most people labor in jobs they hate with their dreams evaporating over the fires that cook their food…backbreaking, uninspired hard work! Back and forth they drudge with a long line of others who struggle to accept a dreary existence.

For some, the desire for creativity captures the heart and hope blooms. Exploration is as sweet and innocent as that first crush. We feel alive again!

Then the idea dawns, "Maybe I could make a living doing what I love?" Awe...and in that moment, seeds of discontent burrow down into the earth of our hearts. We begin to sell our souls for "what might be" in exchange for making the most of "what is." Serenity sprouts wings and flies away.

Aspiring to become a published writer qualifies as my fourth career ambition. This morning I reflect upon some similarities in each of my pursuits, in terms of my struggle to find and define meaning and purpose. Whether fulltime ministry, an arts and crafts business, public education, or the world of publishing, limited positions existed at the top and a whole lot of people aspired to claim them, fierce competition to be sure. This is the appeal of *American Idol*: one from among us common folk makes it to the top!

But what if your destiny does not run parallel with popularity? Can you handle that? I have asked myself this question repeatedly over the years as my path detoured away from positions of power and settled along a reflective and often obscure path. I vividly remember the words of an old salty prophet, Bob Jones, who used to speak to us pastoral leaders twenty years ago, "God is looking for a nameless faceless generation," he warned. We all applauded, but really, who actually wanted to step down from our pulpits of popularity and volunteer for that? Little did I know, at the time, that life would recruit me against my will. I would join the long line of despairing people, trudging along without hope.

In time, my pursuits took me through the world of business, then into the field of education, and finally to this new terrain of aspiring writer. So now, the age-old conflict resurfaces. Can I navigate my way through pursuing my dreams without the drive for success mastering me? Can I retain authenticity as a writer when marketing necessitates self-promotion? Can I be at peace with my purposes if those purposes never catapult me past a small group of people who glean encouragement from my reflections?

One only has to blog for a little while to realize there are a sea of gifted artists, photographers, and aspiring writers; so many talented people, many of whom have devoted an entire lifetime to the craft and yet never made it into that inner circle at the top. What if my only readers are my own circle of friends and acquaintances, who whisper hopeful words back and forth to each other as we go about our lives working our day jobs?

I hesitate to make any pious statements about acceptance when success falls short of the envisioned trophy. Experience has taught me that I will have to eat my words with humility's fork. Just for today, I choose to accept the person I am and the path I currently walk, whether the masses ever read my musings. The funny thing is, though, I like this place of being at peace with my purposes because I have never felt more alive and real!

The pursuit and discovery of destiny is a life-long journey. Often we do not see the intended plan until we look back. Unexpected twists and turns of uncontrollable circumstances often take us down difficult trails. Disappointments riddle our well-intended pursuits, yet when we embrace them, we allow the heart to rest a little easier. In the midst of living life, somehow our destiny eventually makes sense as we process our pain, discover our talents, advance our skills, and plan our goals. Destiny comes to you when you least expect it as you embrace what life sends your way.

A RAINBOW OF POSSIBILITIES

Some of us "creative types" have prism-like minds. Artistic inspiration moves through our thoughts like white light separating into a spectrum of colorful ideas. What may seem a lack of focus to some is, to us, a rainbow of artistic possibilities.

I have always cherished rainbows. During difficult times, rainbows reminded me of hope. I found comfort in knowing that tumultuous life storms would eventually pass. When the clouds do part, even a sliver of sunshine passing through can refract into a breathtakingly beautiful sight. With age comes the understanding that trying on a new identity, career option, or an artistic pursuit often results in feeling fractured. Yet, allowing our minds to bend opportunities into the multiple choices we can sample is essential.

Isaac Newton's prism discovery provides the scientific counterpart of the artist's experience.[5] Light passes through one prism, refracting into a colorful band and then passes through another and becomes white light again. This knowledge gives me hope! Life is a rainbow of possibilities, but then I can refocus all of my efforts into a single project when needed.

This morning I awoke to an email my daughter sent me that features a UCLA course for writers. The course description highlights the publishing world's transformation due to "The Digital Revolution." It emphasizes the need for progressive writers to become technology savvy. Apparently, literary agents and publishing companies expect writers to spend at least five hours

---

5 http://micro.magnet.fsu.edu/primer/java/scienceopticsu/newton/

blogging each week. As I read the description, I chuckled at the irony.

Over the last five years, I have often doubted myself due to my tendency to want it all. My interests in literacy, technology, and the arts made me feel fragmented. I rationalized that pursuing multiple interests was like holding the reins of multiple horses pulling a chariot forward. Now I know this was all preparation for becoming a creative eclectic in this Digital Age.

So for all of you fractured writers/artists out there trying to play technology catch-up, I have started a library of "How to blog" at www.refrainfromtheidentical.com. Check them out under Blogging Screencast Lessons on the right side. I will continue to make them as time permits. I hope these lessons will encourage others who are making the digital transition.

I wrote the following poem after a dream I had about designing a creativity site:

THE EMERGENCE

I am as one grown mute
Puzzle piece of destiny lost
Gaping hole so noticeable
Where voice of hope once snugly fit
Taken from my purpose
In foreign lands of soul to dwell
No longer free to share my faith
Good tidings spoken without restraint
Restore my voice oh God
Return the call to speak your name
Empowered by your Spirit's love
An oracle released from shame

~JoDee Luna

This desire was seeded in my heart in early February 2009, but I did not actually build the site until December 2010...ten months later. I wrote this poem while trying to reconcile feelings of loss from leaving my former life as a missionary. When something new is coming, we often must first grieve the old we leave behind. As I allowed the longing for my previous life to die, the inspiration began for creating a website with the purpose of encouraging others to pursue their creativity. I wanted to provide a plethora of resources for other creative eclectics. I envisioned inspirational writings, artistic projects, and digital designs. I desired to post the inspirational words and creative works of others, as well as restoring my own lost voice.

Our heart seeds desires long before we whisper the prayers! The longing you feel for something more is worth following. Desire precedes change and will often fracture into many possibilities like the vibrant colors of a rainbow. Do not become dismayed by this. A restlessness and indescribable pull will take you in different directions before you understand what is happening. I have noted this reoccurring pattern in my creative life: a creative notion plants itself inside my mind and begins to grow under the surface of conscious thought. If I don't kill the desire by questioning too much, I always end up benefiting from the experience.

I know this tendency to pursue multiple possibilities can become overwhelming. Our minds fill with possibilities while reality stands as a cruel taskmaster over daily affairs. It taunts, "You only have so much time!" Daily we need to prioritize in order to stay focused on what is most important, and regular process writing is so helpful in this. We can weed through our ideas and desires like a prism refocusing into the white light of one project at a time.

REFRAIN FROM THE IDENTICAL

Today is a turning point, having just completed my first manuscript's third edit. Rereading 270 pages repeatedly, as if a first-time reader, was difficult. The first time, I printed out the manuscript and placed it into a three-ring binder. My daughter, Andrea, spent sixteen hours reading every word and making detailed recommendations.

Far from finishing a blossoming writing life, this book merely tips the full pitcher of words spilling from my heart and mind. More manuscripts follow, as exciting to pen as to live. I called my best friend with the news of my rough draft completion and she cheered.

My first blog, created on September 19, 2009, initiated a new world of writing and creating. As of today, March 23, 2010, I have blogged for six months and thoroughly enjoy the process. I envisioned a blog mostly about creativity and ended up with one recording my life. How fitting and in line with my patterns. Capturing the essence of what makes living so special will always be the most creative and meaningful activity I do.

This year I celebrated my fifty years upon this earth. On that special day, I had lunch with three other eclectic artists in my family: my two daughters and my sister. When I look back over the past fifty years, I can say with all certainty that truly, while some of my happiest moments were when I dabbled in artistic projects, ferociously wrote, and digitally designed, none holds a candle to being with the ones I love. If all of my future days could encompass these simple joys, I would be a rich woman indeed.

In pursuing my innate gifting, an encounter with the creative nature of God proved inevitable. I used to wonder what we would do for all eternity in heaven besides worship Him and lay our gifts before His throne. Now I wonder whether the long tables where we will celebrate the marriage supper of the Lamb will also host artistic delights that souls throughout the ages can create next to each other. Not only those who achieved worldly acclaim for their endowed brilliance, but also simple people like you and me who dared to pursue what our Creator imparted in talent and whispered in heart. Perhaps we will sit next to a teen or child and help them try a new craft. I have found nothing upon this earth that shines brighter than the eyes of a child—at any age—when creating.

I welcome you to embrace your artistry as from the Father's heart of love. Seek your own unique destiny, knowing He bestowed the heart of an artist upon you. As I anticipate the end of this long and arduous project, I believe there is a city of faith under construction whose architect and builder is God. During the building of the temple in the Old Testament, God selected artisans and craftspeople to design what only He could envision. I hope to see my life's accomplishments folded into His glorious plan along with all those who dare to *refrain from the identical!*

Acknowledgements

I want to thank Jesus, the Gentle Shepherd of my soul, whose unending creativity miraculously oozes from heaven and falls upon my family and me. I also appreciate the support of my husband, Justin, parents, John and Dee, children, Jason, Andy, Josiah, and Elya, and my best friend, Barbie. They listened to my unending flow of ideas and believed my dreams could come true. A crown in heaven waits because of their undying patience, ability to simplify my infinite perplexities, willingness to read scores of writings, and faithfulness to repeatedly proclaim, "You can!"

I also thank those who helped edit this book: Andrea Luna, Gina Marie Wilson, and Dr. Bonnie Harvey for initial edits. Keidi Keating (The Word Queen) for proofreading. A special thanks to editor Kay Johnson for her substantial revisions that honed content, improved word choice, enhanced tone, and sharpened presentation. Without everyone's help, I never could have finished such a massive and all-consuming project.

ABOUT THE AUTHOR

JoDee Luna grew up in the rural town of Leona Valley nestled between two mountain ranges in southern California. She fondly remembers creative sessions around the kitchen table with her sister and mother. JoDee's life and career path reflect her eclectic nature. She has, at various times, been a missionary, pastor's wife, professional development trainer, digital designer, photographer, sculptor, dancer, artist, classical guitarist, hair stylist, arts and craft business owner, teacher, theatre arts coordinator, ballroom dance teacher, and gardener. She also has a passion for giving back, and she is especially interested in literacy. She has taught grades fifth through eighth and facilitated a middle school literacy program, READ 180, designed by Scholastic Inc., for the last four years.

JoDee savors time with her husband and their four children, their extended family, and their many friends. JoDee has designed an accompanying website, http://www.refrainfromtheidentical.com, intended to build a support community for creative eclectics while providing artistic resources. For her, life is not fully lived without sharing her creativity with others.

www.ingramcontent.com/pod-product-compliance
Lightning Source LLC
Chambersburg PA
CBHW030317290526
45785CB00001B/406